SOUGHT-AFTER

How to **Be Heard, Be Trusted,** and
Be Recognized for Your Expertise

Praise for *Sought-After*

"*Sought-After: How to Be Heard, Be Trusted, and Be Recognized for Your Expertise* is a book about obligation and reward. It is a book about personal renewal. It is a book that invokes individual responsibility and evokes collective achievement. The hardest step, as in most things, is the first. Karen A. Young has created a practical and sustainable guide for those desiring to do what it takes to become sought-after. It is a learning platform, a springboard forward to a future possibility for those willing to see, seize and create opportunity. The building blocks are here. The implementation is up to you."

Steve Gilliland, CSP, CPE, Bestselling Author and Member of the National Speakers Association's Speaker Hall of Fame

"Finally! A handbook on how to get noticed and become "sought after" for your expertise. The business world is filled with countless superstars who have so much to offer but are simply never noticed — kind of like a great product on the market that people just don't know about. Karen A. Young has created the 'roadmap' for those hidden superstars in this book. Real talk, direct, and very actionable. Professionals at every level will benefit from the guidance offered by someone who has truly lived it."

Warren Zeiser, Respected Speaker, Coach, and Consultant for the Nation's Hottest Companies

"After knowing Karen A. Young for years as an HR professional, a pragmatic leader, and a person with intense authenticity, I was not disappointed to find the pages of this book chock-full of practical advice offered from a place of lifelong experience with just the right amount of self-deprecating reference. Karen tells it like it is, with no holding back. *Sought-After* is an authentic, practical, and real-life account of how, while 'mistakes are inevitable, disaster is optional!' Karen has been a constant learner, has surrounded herself with the right people, and has applied the fortitude to use her functional expertise to do the right thing — without the rigidity that is so often associated with subject-matter experts who 'know their stuff' but don't understand the full business contexts of the people they serve. Because Karen has 'been there and done that' on her way from entry-level employee to sought-after expert, her stories about choosing collaboration instead of conflict (after first having made several career-defining and nearly career-ending mistakes) are relatable and applicable for us all. Karen makes the mistakes so that you don't have to. Take it in, make it your own, and fast-track your own 'sought-after' career!"

Amey Sgrignoli, President & CEO, Belco Community Credit Union

"The potential for career-defining moments lies right around every corner. Learn from the masters who will help you shortcut the system, avoid the landmines, and circumvent the roadblocks. *Sought-After* offers the perfect recipe and mindset for long-term career success and professional development. Karen A. Young makes the journey enjoyable, entertaining, and most important, human. Enjoy the ride!"

Paul Falcone, Author, *The Paul Falcone Workplace Leadership Series*

"Karen A. Young provides proof that highly respected leaders are vulnerable and that failure and adversity are key ingredients for making it to the pinnacle of becoming 'sought after.' Karen humorously uses her life's experiences to help readers recognize that our life's learning lessons form the 'what to do' and, more importantly, 'what *not* to do' in a wide range of scenarios. Karen proves that sought-after leaders use their failures to help others avoid similar mistakes!"

Kate Kohler, President, Staub & Associates, LLC (Sandler Training Franchise)

"I have known Karen A. Young since my youth, so imagine my surprise when, years later at a high school reunion, we both discovered we were HR consultants — her in PA and me in TX. It has been a joy reconnecting and sharing the highs and lows of HR and self-employment. She is the consummate professional and, as everyone knows, HR knows not only where the bodies are buried, but who dug the holes!! Karen is generous in sharing her knowledge (but is probably taking big secrets to her own grave). Her writing is insightful and this newest book offers perspectives about workplace and life success. She is truly someone who is heard, trusted, and recognized for her expertise. There's no one better to share secrets of success (but NEVER those deep, dark HR secrets)."

Terri Swain, Chief Truth Seeker, DecipHR Investigators
Chief Human, The HR Consultant

"Karen A. Young, a successful HR professional and entrepreneur, uses insights from her experiences to provide the reader with compelling tales of learning, plus reflection opportunities, moments for renewal, and sound recommendations. After reading this book, you will gain additional insights into yourself as a professional and you will be equipped to attract new opportunities as a result of learning how to navigate and persist more effectively in your craft — so that you may be 'sought after' professionally on a regular basis."

John J. "Ski" Sygielski, President, HACC, Central Pennsylvania's Community College

"I first met Karen Young at a training shortly after she founded HR Resolutions. She inspired me then with the clarifying question, 'What else do you need from me to be successful in this task?" and has been a great friend and mentor since. When I stepped into my first HR Director role, her sage advice was, 'Don't change anything for 90 days. And do an I-9 audit.' I took that advice to every organization thereafter. In her writing, you will see yourself as your career has evolved, you will laugh as you read about her Career-Defining Moments, and you will reflect on your current level of influence. This book can be given to a young professional in their journey to the C-suite or to realize their professional dreams. Practical, honest, and funny, Karen's voice shines through with unique authenticity."

Sara Kennedy, Senior Vice President for Associate Experience, Members 1st Federal Credit Union

SOUGHT-AFTER

How to **Be Heard**, **Be Trusted**, and **Be Recognized** for Your Expertise

KAREN A. YOUNG

With a foreword by Steve Gilliland,
Bestselling Author and Member of the
National Speakers Association's Speaker Hall of Fame

SILVER TREE
PUBLISHING

Editing by:
Kate Colbert

Cover design and typesetting by:
George Stevens

First edition, March 2023

Paperback ISBN: 978-1-948238-43-4
Hardcover ISBN: 978-1-948238-44-1
Library of Congress Control Number: 2023904157

Created in the United States of America

Dedication

This book is dedicated to my best friend and better half, Barry Young. My husband, Barry, is literally the best husband ever (yes, we should put that on a coffee mug) and he is the best part of me. After I published my first book, now reimagined and republished as *Honest and Real: An Essential Guidebook for Drama-free Human Resources*, Barry teased me about being #3 in the book's acknowledgements section (come on — he followed God and my parents!). We've had some good laughs about that, and he does know that (next to God) he is #1 in my heart, mind, and soul.

Before I was "sought-after" in my career and in the human resources industry, Barry "sought after" me — many years ago, when we were both in graduate school. He encouraged me to start my own business, and he handles everything (and I mean *everything*) at the house so that I can focus on my joy — work, writing, and speaking. Don't get me wrong ... Barry is human, and so am I. We've had the typical marital spats over the years, few and far between. But I only remember all the joy. Barry has held me when I've cried and celebrated with me when I've achieved personal and professional successes. He has been relentless in his support and love of me through two cancer treatments. And he didn't blink once when I decided upon a double mastectomy to better ensure my future health and peace of mind.

Barry and I are rarely apart, and I miss him like oxygen when we are separated. We are blessed in our lives together and we do our best to make everything an adventure. This book, like so much of what I have to offer the world, is only possible because of him.

Snook — This one's for you! ❤

Contents

Foreword

By Steve Gilliland, Bestselling Author and Member of the
National Speakers Association's Speaker Hall of Fame

Sought-After: How to Be Heard, Be Trusted, and Be Recognized for Your Expertise is a book about obligation and reward. It is a book about personal renewal. It is a book that invokes individual responsibility and evokes collective achievement.

The hardest step, as in most things, is the first. In bringing you this remarkable book, Karen A. Young has created a practical and sustainable guide for those desiring to do what it takes to become sought-after. The framework in *Sought-After* is a learning platform or foundation — a springboard forward to a future possibility for those willing to see, seize, and create opportunity.

In the pages that follow, Karen dares you to ask yourself: "Are you ready to assume accountability for what it takes to be heard, trusted, and recognized for your endeavors and expertise — to do the work and then be visible and approachable in ways that may influence the entire course of your life and career?" The building blocks are here. The implementation is up to you.

Sought-After: How to Be Heard, Be Trusted, and Be Recognized for Your Expertise is a rare, indispensable resource for those determined to make the best of their careers. This book isn't for those who think they know it all nor is it for those unwilling to do the work. Curious learners find the courage to apply what is of value in the furtherance of their careers. They express gratitude and appreciation for the chance to change today with what they learned from yesterday. This book is a moment to learn.

If you want to be heard, trusted, recognized, and respected in your current organization and beyond, there is a path for getting there; Karen shows you the way. In this book, she outlines several key strategies of engagement that are tried, true, and tested from the crucible of her own personal experience and from case studies of sought-after experts she has met along the way. Through hard-won lessons, she shares the goal of advancement for those willing to step forward and become vital contributors to their own success.

Ultimately, we can stumble forward blindly — blaming circumstance, condition, or fate as tangible factors in the outcomes of our professional and personal pursuits. Or we can become aware, regain our accountability, and move beyond the excuses of past conditions that must no longer define us.

Of course, you have perhaps found — as most of us have — that life sometimes supports those who coast and select the "easy" route, but it rewards those who overcome the difficulty. Growth comes from meeting a new challenge, and confident competence ensues from exceeding the challenge's demands. Difficulty — like the hard work required to become sought-after in your profession or your organization — is often temporary and not as difficult as we initially fear ... but the chronic discomfort of accepting average (or less than average) in your life and work can become permanent.

Today, you take the personal challenge and become *"sought after, heard, trusted, and recognized for your expertise."*

All the best,

Steve Gilliland
Bestselling Author and Member of the National Speakers Association's Speaker Hall of Fame

Ready to become SOUGHT-AFTER?

Follow the path that has worked for many experts who have become trusted advisors and highly regarded guides to people, organizations, audiences, and entire industries. Think of the building blocks as taking you higher in your influence and vantage point, or further along a career path. Start with yourself and your own expertise, then get moving and keep climbing!

The four building blocks for becoming sought-after:

➤ Know *your* stuff

➤ Know *their* stuff

➤ Know the *audience*

➤ Be *flexible.*

Letter to the Reader

Dear Reader:

By the time you read this, the journey I have taken in writing this book for you has either been cathartic for me or it has created even *more* PTSD regarding all the Career-Ending Moves (CEMs) I've made! It takes courage (and, admittedly, a little insanity!) to write a book in which you tell your deepest, darkest career secrets. But my mistakes in the early years of my career — even the ones that were job-ending moves and threatened to be what I call *Career*-Ending Moves (CEMs) — are instructive. Later on, as you and I get to know each other better through the pages of this book, I will reframe those Career-*ending* Moves to "Career-*Defining* Moments." Indeed, it's all in what you do with a negative situation after it happens. If you can learn from any of my past mistakes and workplace dramas, then I will have served you well in writing this book.

This book is exactly what the title implies. *Sought-After: What it Takes to Be Heard, Be Trusted, and Be Recognized for Your Expertise.* In the chapters that follow, I will present you with four building blocks to

Here's Your First Challenge

If you are brave, jump ahead to the end of the book and complete the "Scenarios Exercises" as your mind interprets them and would respond to them *today*. Don't try to guess what I would want you to say *after* you master the art of being sought-after. Just be you — truthfully, unapologetically, and confidently.

Then come back to the beginning of the book and immerse yourself in the learning. Forget about the little "pre-test" you just took. And finally, when you finish the book, re-do the exercises, and see if and how your responses might have changed. Perhaps they remained the same — and there's nothing wrong with that at all. But *maybe* the book will enable you to see workplace situations in a new and different way. Feel free to mark this book up: Write in it, dog-ear it, make it yours. This is your workbook for YOU — and no one else. (Unless you find the transformation so exciting that you want to snap a photo and share it on LinkedIn with other *Sought-After* readers. Far be it from me to stop you from sharing your experience with others and giving the book some free public relations!)

set you up to be "Sought-After." This is *not* a "how to" book. Each of the building blocks that will help you climb to the pinnacle height of being sought-after must be evaluated, reviewed, chewed upon, and implemented by the uniqueness of *you*. You may have Building Block 4 nailed already and could lead Change Management in your sleep. If so, that's great. Regardless of your perceived expertise and confidence as it relates to each of the building blocks in the Sought-After Framework, be sure to read each section of the book. The sections devoted to your areas of strength will either reinforce what you are already doing and give you some positive affirmation *or* you may gain further insight into your approaches, beliefs, and processes that might help you level-up your performance.

> **This is *not* a "how to" book. Each of the building blocks that will help you climb to the pinnacle height of being sought-after needs to be evaluated, reviewed, chewed upon, and implemented by the uniqueness of *you*.**

If you work for bad leaders, this book is *not* a cure-all. But it will help *you* become a better leader (and your own performance and contributions at work are at least half the battle when it comes to workplace effectiveness and job satisfaction). The lessons in this book will help you make a difference where other leaders may not. It will affirm *your* good work when working on self-improvement, business acumen, communication skills, or change management. What's more, the ideas in this book will make you more marketable when you're ready to make a job or career change. Yes, even key leaders leave employers because of poor leadership — it's not just middle managers and entry-level employees who get fed up with poor leadership and toxic cultures! Never be afraid to seek greener pastures — the success stories of many people who are sought-after involve the pivotal decisions to leave organizations and managers behind.

If you are lucky enough to work for great leaders, they are likely to reinforce and praise you for the subtle changes you may make when you begin embracing and acting upon the concepts and suggestions you'll find in this book. Turn to these leaders for mentorship and input. Demonstrate your interest in mirroring their best traits and skills. Seek their insights on the sections in the book that you'd like to share with them. And, if they disagree with me, that's OK. Be open to accepting constructive criticism — it can only make you stronger. Also be willing to respectfully disagree with their insights.

None of us has all the answers. Some of us come closer than others. All of us can gain new insights to improve the trajectory of our own careers. I sincerely hope I am one of the people in your life and work who "comes closer" for you. This book is for *you*. I've "been there, done that" — and now I want to share the lessons that helped me along the way, knowing these lessons might help you too. For me — just as it is for you — the learning and leading journey continues. I still strive to learn every day. I hope you do too. Because there is always a (slightly or drastically) different approach I can take. And, you know what? *I still make mistakes.* Some of them comical; some of them painful. Fortunately, Career-Ending Moves are fewer and farther between for me these days!

All the best,

Karen A. Young, *Always a work in progress!*

CHAPTER 1

The Journey

"OMG – it's a blank page," I thought as I started to write this book, the blinking cursor on the bright-white screen mocking me. What do I write that *you* want to read? I was momentarily intellectually paralyzed.

With any project, as it is for many people, the most difficult point is staring at the blank page and pondering, *"Where do I begin?"* There are a lot of cliches about motivation, inertia, and getting started on a big, ambitious, audacious project:

"How do you eat an elephant? One bite at a time."

"Begin at the beginning."

"Just close your eyes and leap!"

The cheerleading is all well and great *until* that project is staring you in the face ... and the page is blank! But here we are, and there are more than 100 words in this chapter already, and I'm feeling less afraid. We can do this. And we can do this together. I've started out vulnerably (and maybe a little awkwardly). Because the truth of the matter is that no matter where you are in your career — entry-level newbie, disoriented career changer, rain-making ladder-climber, or organizational and industry rock star — the journey is humbling and personal. And your story is just beginning. Yes, even if you are already — by every reasonable measure — "sought-after." Because there are always ways to be more valued, better heard, better respected, and more widely recognized — by the right people and organizations at the right time — for your expertise.

As I mentioned in my Letter to the Reader, I'm still a work in progress ... and always will be. So, even though I've climbed my way to the top of a few corporate ladders, have written a couple of pretty good books, and these days find myself being sought out by people and organizations that "wow" me, I'm still learning. My story is still evolving. This book, in many ways, is about stories — about yours and mine. In the pages that follow, I'll share stories from my career (and from the careers of other people I interviewed) that illustrate what it takes to be "sought-after." Keep in mind that my own stories are from the world of human resources (HR) — that's my experience. But the premise of the stories applies to any professional looking to be sought-after and heard. Whether you are in HR, marketing, finance, operations, clinical healthcare, the arts, the practice of law ...the concepts in this book will work. But career success doesn't happen overnight — it's a *journey*. It takes time, effort, heartache, and even literal "blood, sweat, and tears." Then one day you will step out of a meeting and say to yourself, "Well, what do you know?! *They* came to *me* for a change! Everyone was listening to *me* and wanting to hear more."

Career success doesn't happen overnight — it's a *journey*.

Stumbling Into My Profession

How did I become a trusted advisor who people seek out? One step at a time (and sometimes two steps forward and one step back.) These days, people listen to me – heck, they pay me for my advice and counsel (just as you did when you bought this book)! And some days, I can hardly believe it ... or believe I deserve it. Indeed, imposter syndrome strikes here; I'm just a simple girl from Harrisburg, PA! Unless we were born with silver spoons in our mouths and with the benefit of nepotism to allow us to "hold court" with audiences and colleagues even if we don't deserve it (and I'm guessing those folks aren't reading this book!), we all have humble beginnings. For me, it has not been an easy road. In fact, the road has been bumpy, and the roadblocks have been frequent. Many of the roadblocks have been self-imposed. (Have you ever found you are getting in your own way? Yep, me too!) Today, I am the proud founder and president of a boutique consulting firm called HR Resolutions. We provide human resources support to multiple companies, and we *love* what we do. But believe me — I have *not* always been "sought-after!" I haven't even always been seen.

If you have read my previous book, *Honest and Real: An Essential Guidebook to Drama-Free Human Resources*, you already know a little bit about me — how I stumbled into the world of human resources and how I made some epic, memorable mistakes as I was climbing the corporate ladder. Some of the stories that follow in this chapter might sound familiar, though I assure you that the lessons will be applied differently in this book. And if *Sought-After* is the first of my books that you have generously picked up (thank you for your trust!), what I'm about to share might make you laugh. Or cringe. Or feel a little less alone.

So here goes! Let's begin at the beginning!

I stumbled into my profession.

Back in my undergraduate days (I like to refer to them as the "dark ages"), there was no such thing as a human resources "academic major" or degree. I was going to be a classical pianist who ... well, I don't have the foggiest idea what I was going to do with that education and expertise. But I *had* to go to college, according to my parents. Music was the only thing I knew, and piano was my specialty.

I grew up being *the best* musician in junior- and senior-high. I didn't even have to work hard at it; what happened when I sat down at a piano was the result of natural talent. Well, then I got to college. Guess what? I was surrounded by a whole group of *the best* musicians ... I was no longer *the* best. I was good but I no longer stood out. *"Now what?"* I wondered. When you couldn't cut it as a music major at Lebanon Valley College, you transitioned to the elementary-education track (oh wait, I would still be teaching music, and music had just broken my heart) or you became a business major. Being done with music, I figured that business administration would be easy-peasy, so I made the leap to a new major.

One of my electives during the second semester of my freshman year was organizational psychology. Hmm, not only was the business track easy for me, but it was also intriguing! Organizational psychology was all about human behavior at work — on teams and in organizations ... among and between bosses and employees. It was about a different kind of "ensemble," all trying to work in harmony. I loved it immediately. You may have read about these workplace studies where organizational psychologists would come into manufacturing plants and apply stop watches to the workers to motivate and measure their efficiency. Ugh, I'm much more people-friendly than that. Thankfully, organizational psychology also looks at the balance between life, work, home, and the person. (No offense to those time-measuring people — they provide some pretty useful data. And I've always appreciated a metronome.)

Business administration and organizational psychology. Voila! I had found my career. Again, there was no such thing as a human resources degree, so I added psychology as a second major. Organizational psychology, alongside the study of business, was a good fit for me because it looks at processes and improvements. To this day, I still review, analyze, evaluate, and seek to improve processes — for the sake of increasing efficiencies, improving cultures, and generally improving workplaces for the good of the employer *and* the employees.

So, what happened when I finished college and wanted to take all that HR, biz admin, and organizational psych know-how out into the big, bad world? Well, the next part of the journey wasn't easy. It was incredibly difficult to get a job in personnel (what everyone called HR before it was HR) unless you had experience. How do you gain experience in a profession if you can't get a first job in that profession? (Here's where the journey really begins ...) You make your own experience!

How do you gain experience in a profession if you can't get a first job in that profession? (Here's where the journey really begins ...) You make your own experience!

On-the-Job Training — For Better and for Worse

My first "real" job after college was as an assistant manager with Wendy's. (Don't you *dare* say "ugh" — I learned a *lot* in fast food, and it paid well too!) Assistant Manager responsibilities:

- Scheduling

- Hiring/firing

- Pay increases

- Managing (teenagers)

- Performance evaluations

- Discipline

- Employee relations

- Training

- Interpreting policies/procedures.

Interesting ... sounds like the responsibilities of a personnel/human resources manager. I made my own experience in HR by accepting responsibility for all the restaurant tasks that involved HR duties. Many of my peers didn't want those responsibilities anyway — who likes HR, right?

I was never promoted beyond the role of assistant manager with Wendy's. Not being shy, I asked a district manager what was holding me back. His answer? I was too honest when asked how things were going. *What? Too honest?*[1] Apparently, when asked how things were going, I was supposed to say "great!" regardless of anything that was *realistically* holding our restaurant back — where we just might want some guidance from a regional perspective. I was supposed to conform, blend in, be quiet. Apparently, I didn't yet know how to be *heard* by a leader.

---

1   Go figure. Leave it to me to end up writing a book entitled *Honest and Real: An Essential Guidebook for Drama-Free Human Resources*. I still believe in honesty. And I have learned how to pair it with diplomacy and compassion for better results than I generated earlier in my career.

My next opportunity, when it was time to get out of the quick-serve restaurant business, was still *not* in HR, per se. But I continued to accept HR-like responsibilities as the front-office manager of a hotel. There, I added more skills to the experience bucket — like learning to collaborate with other operational departments to fulfill the mission of the organization. I was branching out and I was learning to speak and listen on behalf of our people and our business. I didn't know it then, but I was already on my way to earning a seat at the table and a voice in the conversation.

Finally, my next job was a *real* human resources job (for a competitor of Blockbuster Video.) I was a young woman (who still felt a lot like a little girl) with big dreams — and I was moving to the big city of Philadelphia for my first career job. It was so exciting; I had "made" it. *Oh, little girl, how silly you were!*

Philadelphia was to be my new home *and* the scene of the crime, as it were, for my first "Career-Ending Move" (CEM).[2] You've heard of "trial by fire" and "learning the hard way," and that I did when I arrived in Philly. My boyfriend at the time also worked in the video rental business; he owned an adult video store. As it turned out, my new employer thought my relationship with the owner of such a competing (but arguably very different) store posed a potential conflict of interest and he also found it "morally" objectionable. "What if our customers knew about the kind of video business your boyfriend owns?" he thought. My career-ending move (CEM) was the moment that I blabbed my mouth about my boyfriend's company to a teenage employee at one of the company's stores (because I was trying to be cool). And that was the beginning of the end. "You know Karen … the new girl? Her boyfriend runs an *adult* video store!" turned into an entire company-wide watercooler rumor mill. In no time flat, everyone knew the gossip and they knew I had started the gossip all by myself. My judgment and my connections were called into question, and it was over. My "dream" career job lasted less than three months — welcome to "employment at will!"

---

2   There is an entire chapter of this book devoted to CEMs. That's how important they can be to the journey!

My judgment and my connections were called into question, and it was over. My "dream" career job lasted less than three months — welcome to "employment at will!"

That's OK — I was young and resilient. I was also living in Philadelphia with student loans, rent, car payments, and bills. I needed a job! On to my next "career" job — working as a temporary payroll clerk for a restaurant-holding company. It was too much fun; my new job was in Center City with a train commute, cool restaurants, and "hip" people to work with. Their personnel files consisted of the torn-off portion of the W-4 sent to "corporate" … with the new employee's pay rate written on the form. Once again, creating my own experience, not only did I process their payrolls, but I created their first HR Department.

Along comes the next "oops!"

Back in the aforementioned "dark ages," payrolls were processed on paper! (This was shortly after dinosaurs roamed the earth.) I had exactly *one* training session with the prior payroll person before she happily went off to greener pastures. (Remember though — I was young, and I knew *everything*.) Piece of cake — you put numbers on a green bar ledger paper [3] and phone it in.

Reflection Question

When have you created your own experience? Maybe you negotiated your way into the creation of a new role for yourself or maybe you found a way to turn "no" into "why not?" Perhaps you ventured into the unknown, only to find out that exciting possibilities exist on the other side of fear.

Take a moment to reflect upon the opportunities you manifested into reality by proving your worth, taking risks, and asking for someone's trust. What lessons have you learned through these "choose your own adventure" moments in your career … and is it time, once again, to create your own experience? Go ahead — leap!

---

3   https://www.amazon.com/Wilson-Jones-Columnar-Columns-WG50-24A/dp/B000EUJ0WU

Literally, *phone it into* the bank, who would calculate wages and taxes, and then produce the checks. (Yeah, no direct deposit yet. LOL!)

I was back in the restaurant industry — this time in a payroll/HR role instead of managing a quick-serve restaurant. And the restaurants I worked on behalf of now had table service and therefore their servers earned, you guessed it, *tips*! Now, tip payments are challenging in any environment, even today. Some are actually paid out by the employer on the paycheck; some were already received by the employee at the time of the restaurant patrons giving the "tips" and just needed to be recorded later for tax purposes. My first solo payroll processing just happened to be the payout for the largest catering event the company had ever held. Lots of people working; lots of tips. Well … I double-paid the tips for *every single server who had worked the event.* (Boy, was I about to be popular with the servers!) Fortunately (and this piece is critical to the story), I realized my mistake before paychecks were distributed.

I was convinced that my newfound "second chance" in my profession was over even faster than the first one. I still, to this day, remember walking into the controller's office with my head hung low. I told him I had made a very serious error in the payroll, explaining that every server was paid 200% of their actual tips. He rolled his chair back, kicked his feet up on his desk and said, "So, how are you going to fix it?" I explained my idea, admitted that we would not be able to recoup it all because some of the servers were "this pay only" — meaning this was their first and last catering job for the company. His answer? "Great. Make it happen." I was sitting in the chair across from his desk and I didn't hop right up to leave. So, he asked me what was wrong. "I still have my job? This was major." He said, "Of course …" then proceeded to explain that I wasn't being fired over this mistake because:

1. The mistake was identified in advance of the mistake becoming a public catastrophe.

2. No excuses were given. I owned up to the mistake as soon as I realized what I had done.

3. There was a plan to fix it! And we both felt confident that this kind of mistake would never happen again.

As I type this, I still get goosebumps over that moment in time. The way the controller handled that incident was one of the most gracious and reinforcing things a leader had *ever* done for me. I hope I continue to honor him by applying that same philosophy with my direct reports — allowing employees to help create the solution or damage control in the wake of a problem or mistake, and ensuring they know that I trust them, that I understand that mistakes happen, and that I appreciate their honesty and ownership of the error.

I still remember that payroll position fondly. I stayed there for a bit until it was time to come home to Harrisburg. (OK, my boyfriend and I broke up … and I came home with my tail between my legs, but that is a completely different story for another kind of book!)

Returning to Harrisburg, I finally had that coveted "HR" experience (mostly). The next element of HR that I wanted to tackle? Recruiting. My first position back in this distinct area of human resources was as a professional services recruiter for the Byrnes Group, a small head-hunting firm in South Central Pennsylvania, not far from my home-town. Who knew that working as a "headhunter" was more sales than recruiting? I figured "what the heck — I can do this." And I learned as I went. As a recruiter, I got to interview people, create job postings, help companies decide who they really needed to hire, and make connections helping companies and people find a good match. Much like the experi-ences from fast food, this was a good learning opportunity; I still apply the ad-writing skills I learned back then to today's market. And it turns out that I also had a knack for sales. Who knew? But because I was young and dumb, another "career-ending move" was inevitably just around the corner. After an "oops" with the Byrnes group (I got caught looking for another job on company time), I was on the hunt to make the right company/employee match for *myself* yet again.

Welcome to Human Resources

As luck (and hard work and tenacity) would have it, I landed my first *for-real* HR job as a payroll and personnel specialist with Harrisburg Paper Company, a supplies distribution division of International Paper Company. Believe it or not, I found this job through the unemployment office. (There are diamonds in the rough through their career boards — give it a chance.) During my eight-year tenure with Harrisburg Paper, I accomplished a great deal, professionally and personally. I:

- ✦ Achieved my certification as an HR Professional through the HR Certification Institute

- ✦ Earned my master's degree in industrial relations

- ✦ Met and married my husband, Barry

- ✦ Was promoted multiple times, ending in a corporate-headquarters position

- ✦ Led HR in multiple locations with different unions

- ✦ Created a selection process for post-acquisition staffing decisions that was utilized across the country

- ✦ Was a PITA (pain-in-the-ass) to supervisors and leaders (sorry Phyllis, not sorry Tom!)

- ✦ Had many "oops" moments (more on these through the rest of the book ... I promise!).

Leaving that company was one of the hardest career decisions I ever made. That company "made me" — it's where I learned and grew, practiced new skills, and continually challenged myself to be better. There, I developed the core competencies and attitudes that have made me the HR professional and the leader I am today. When I look back at my time at Harrisburg Paper Company, I realize that this book would not be possible if not for that career experience. The basis of *Sought-After*'s four building blocks started with that job. What an amazing experience — and it all started for me as Ted Lick's "payroll girl!" (Oh, I remember how much I loved/hated that descriptor!)

Leaving Harrisburg Paper Company gave me the opportunity to gain more professional experience by transitioning from a distribution/sales environment into a manufacturing environment — which, by the way, is difficult to break into if you don't have manufacturing experience. (See the initial HR quandary — how do you get HR experience if you can't get into HR ...?

My career has been full of chicken/egg dilemmas!) The position was landed by demonstrating how people skills are transferable, regardless of the industry. Thompson Industries hired me as their new HR manager! There are many lessons that I learned in my new role in the big, bad world of manufacturing but my favorite story involves the first time I met with the union reps at the plant. I have a feeling they remember me too!

Picture this: I'm in my new office and these two gentlemen walk in, introduce themselves, and sit down. This was the start of 2nd shift. My working hours enabled me to see both first and second shift. I was about to wrap up my own workday and these guys didn't have an appointment with me; they just left the factory floor shortly after the start of their shift and came into my office. Now, I am always a courteous person and welcoming of anyone who breezes through my office door, but I also understand that if you're a frontline factory worker and you're not on the plant floor, your work is not getting done (and we're paying you to work, so ...). I promptly, and politely, told them to get back to work on the floor. The looks on their faces were priceless — no one had ever spoken to them that way when performing their union duties. Yes, they returned to the plant floor. (After about five minutes, I went out on the floor to meet with them.) From that moment on, we had an excellent working relationship with appropriate boundaries. We established our mutual expectations that first day and, even in dealing with future grievances, we were able to work through them in a manner that was fair and appropriate for both parties. I believe we always delivered such good results because of the respect we established with each other from the start of our relationship.

I was working this job when the North American Free Trade Act (NAFTA) was enacted. These were interesting times in manufacturing, to say the least. Thompson Industries was a steel manufacturer, who chose to move 50% of our plant's work to Mexico. I must admit, professionally, this was one of the most difficult times I'd yet had from the perspective of advocating for our people while marching along with orders regarding the future of the company. I found it difficult to reconcile the needs of the business with the needs of the employees. I struggled. At the end of the day, I delivered on the directives of the business, *but* I allowed my human side to show through. I cried right along with the union members when the announcement was made. (I don't know if that was right or wrong, but it was what it was! What was happening in our business was very personal — for employees and for their families.)

When all was said and done, my position was eliminated too. It was determined that there was no need for an HR director when 50% of the work was out of the country. I wished everyone well, and hoped we'd all bounce back — personally and professionally. As for how the company did with its manufacturing operations in Mexico? Well, the move to Mexico didn't go so well ... it turns out that steel rusts when it comes across the Rockies. Who knew?!

So, what happened to me next, in my long and winding trajectory from "not really an HR person yet" to "HR leader" and eventually sought-after advisor? I'm glad you asked! We have arrived, my readers, at the last of the "corporate" jobs I would take on before striking out on my own to create my beloved business, HR Resolutions. This final corporate gig, at a company we'll call Magical Bubbles, Inc., really led me to a key moment of growth and professional impasse. It was here that I discovered that I should be heard, I should be trusted, and I should be recognized for my expertise. *None* of those things happened in this position!

A few of the highlights of my experience with Magical Bubbles, Inc. (names have been changed to, well, you know):

- ✦ On Day 1, I discovered that my peers didn't know I was coming ("Karen who?")

- ✦ I was provided neither a computer, nor an email address, nor a phone for the first three days of my employment (So much for hitting the ground running!)

- ✦ I had to self-learn a trademarked training program and facilitate the training of others on bootlegged copies of the documentation

- ✦ I was directed to *not* report a workers' comp injury and to disallow the employee to go for medical treatment for their workplace injury

- ✦ My manager was so prone to treating employees like liars and cheats that he refused to believe I had appendicitis until my husband called to let him know I was being wheeled into surgery

- → I was called back to work before I was medically released from that emergency surgery

- → I received a written warning for my "lack of people skills" after the organizational safety statistics were issued, indicating we had three lost-time accidents (when the plant supposedly "never" had any such accidents with the prior HR manager). A lost-time accident is a serious workplace injury resulting in an employee being unable to work for a period of time; these accidents are considered the second-most serious workplace injuries, behind fatalities.

- → I received a final warning for my "lack of people skills" when the plant manager didn't receive a portion of his year-end bonus because accidents were reported (and, well, it's not so much that anyone cared that people had accidents at the company … they just cared about maintaining the illusion that accidents never happened).

The beginning of the end for me at Magical Bubbles was when I got called back to work before being medically released after my surgery. My body was healing, and I was in pain, but they "needed" me. So, I showed up. I am a firm believer that everything happens for a reason, though I can't say that those reasons were always obvious in the moment. I was called back to "hostess" an outside trainer for a companywide seminar we were holding about workplace morale. (Oh, the irony!) Well, the presenter that I was hosting was also a business coach for small-business start-ups. Hmmm … I had an idea for a start-up too. A few months later, I reached out to him to talk about this idea I had (the birth of HR Resolutions!). I hired Glen to help me get my idea off the ground. My goal was to have my first client by the end of a four-month engagement with Glen and he agreed to help make that happen; the finish line would have been January 31, 2005. I didn't expect to be able to jump ship from my corporate job by February 2005 — I envisioned that as the start of a side hustle that would eventually become my full-time effort. Juggling my job and my start-up was exciting and exhausting. And *never* did I do HR Resolutions' work on my employer's time; all my solopreneur work took place on evenings and weekends (my time!) or during lunch breaks (I often attended networking events at the lunch hour).

I was fired from Magical Bubbles on January 14, 2005, because of my "lack of people skills" (the day after bonuses were announced!). The very first thing I did — before I even called my husband — was call Glen. He asked me what I was crying about — he insisted that being set free from my day job was "great news?" I asked him to give me 10 minutes to wrap my head around the whole thing. (No one likes to be fired, no matter what!) But I knew that Glen was right, even as I was coping with the panic of "I just lost my job!" Glen hung up on me and called me back in 10 minutes. His question for me: "Are you over it now?" Through his coaching and support, I had my first signed contract for HR Resolutions on January 17, 2005 – three days after being fired and 14 days before my self-imposed deadline for landing my first client!

Suddenly and finally, someone was choosing me. Not to be an employee and a powerless "worker bee" but to be a trusted advisor. I was being "sought after."

And you can be too. No matter where you've been and where you are in your career, there is always the possibility — if you do the work and you stay the course — to develop the kind of expertise that leads to respect and demand. You know it and I know it ... and now it's time for you to claim it and get started on the four-step process for becoming sought-after. The following chapters will show you how.

> **No matter where you've been and where you are in your career, there is always the possibility — if you do the work and you stay the course — to develop the kind of expertise that leads to respect and demand.**

Right now, you might not be finding yourself at the top of the "trusted advisor" list for the people you want to serve. And that's OK. Wherever you are today is a good place to start. And try not to let that dreaded "imposter syndrome" slow you down. You *should* be heard; you *should* be trusted; you *should* be recognized for your expertise. No matter what someone else says or does! As my friend and colleague (and sought-after expert!) Kate Colbert says: "Don't let someone else take your sparkle! Stand up and shine!"

As you'll see while we explore the *Sought-After* framework together, there is hard work ahead. You will need to put in the work — the intellectual work, the leg work, the interpersonal work, and the emotional work — to get there. Nothing was handed to me and, while I hope it may happen for you, it's unlikely that being heard, being trusted, and being recognized will be handed to you either. Earning it, as it turns out, is what makes it so sweet.

CHAPTER 2

Career-Ending Moves

Let's talk about what I call "career-ending moves." This phrase even merits an entry in the *Urban Dictionary*![4] How cool is that? (Every now and then, I'm pretty hip.) When I talk about career-ending moves, I'm not referring to the type of career-ending move (CEM) where you're *choosing* to end your career (or at least tempting fate), like when you tell your boss to shove it and then you get fired. I'm talking about the kind of moves (behaviors, decisions, regretful utterances) that make you go, "Hmmm — what was I thinking?" Frankly, you probably won't even realize you've had a CEM until it's too late. Additionally, they could turn out to just be career-stalling moves (I hope). In writing this book, I believe there are "career bloopers" also — not as "career threatening" as CEMs. Steve Gilliland, the world-renowned (ahem, "sought-after") speaker and author who penned the foreword for this book, believes CEMs are more likely caused by bad decisions. We all make mistakes — some, according to Gilliland, "are larger than others." Author and entrepreneur Kate Colbert adds, "Don't let a mistake define you, even if it was a big one." All the experts I interviewed for this book talked about getting out in front of your mistake as soon as it's discovered. To err is human, to grow from it is divine. (Well, maybe not divine. But to growth through and past our mistakes is certainly ideal. Everyone who has ever ascended to a place of true, earned leadership has spent a good deal of time reflecting on their mistakes.)

---

4   https://www.urbandictionary.com/define.php?term=career-ending%20move *(Warning: explicit language.)*

Don't Take My Word for It!

Throughout this book, I share stories and advice from a few truly successful and avidly sought-after professionals. Because I'm just one voice and you deserve many. I hope you'll enjoy hearing from this cast of characters as much as I have enjoyed learning from them — before, during, and after their interviews for *Sought-After*. The people I'll be introducing you to — all of whom I have sought after for advice or professional services — include:

- **Kate Colbert:** Renowned marketing expert, communications coach, researcher, and speaker; successful small-business founder and owner; and bestselling author of the books *Think Like a Marketer: How a Shift in Mindset Can Change Everything for Your Business* and *Commencement: The Beginning of a New Era in Higher Education.*

- **John Dame:** Business strategist, CEO coach, author, and master Vistage chair. He is in-demand for his insightful, and realistic, approach to strategic planning and has created the "Evolution Leadership Conference Series." John understands the risks and challenges that CEOs and leaders must face and provides planning tools enabling them to execute faster for quicker results.

- **Steve Gilliland:** National Speakers Association's Hall of Fame speaker and one of the most in-demand (i.e., sought-after!) and top-rated speakers in the world. Recognized as a master storyteller and brilliant comedian, he can be heard on SiriusXM Radio's Laugh USA and Blue Collar Radio. Steve works to build others up through his presentations and books.

- **Ed Staub:** Sales, leadership, and culture expert; renowned trainer and author; and retired co-owner of the highest-performing Sandler Franchise, Staub & Associates. He released the book *Life of Balance vs. Imbalance* in 2022. Ed's career has been focused on building and developing relationships and demonstrating "trusted advisor" in everything he has accomplished in his career.

Mistakes are inevitable; disaster is optional. I believe that it's entirely up to you whether you have a career interruption, a painful aftermath, or a permanent career demise after a mistake or misstep is made. Even people who are the very best at what they do are bound to have stories about where they've screwed up along the way. Ask yourself: What have you done in your professional past that you have looked back on, grimaced at the memory, and thought "Hmmm?" I encourage you to look deeply at these moments and challenge yourself to own them and learn from them — like I have in my stories throughout this book. Oh yes, have no fear, I am still embarrassed by some of the stunts I pulled way back when. But what is critical is that not a single "career-ending move" has ever been repeated! I'm the poster child for "Live and learn."

What have you done in your professional past that you have looked back on, grimaced at the memory, and thought "Hmmm?"

Why Are Career-Ending Moves So Important?

CEMs can and should be career-*defining* for you, as opposed to career-*ending*. Upon reflection, after something has gone seriously sideways for you at work, you should be able to determine:

1. What you'll do in the situation, and

2. What you'll do next (both in the moment and in the greater picture).

Please don't allow your mistakes — painful and embarrassing as they may be — to determine your self-worth. You are more than those moments, especially if you have learned from them. In fact, being sought-after shouldn't define your self-worth either. Whether people hang on your every last word, trust you implicitly, and consider you a "household name" (i.e., whether you are sought-after by the definition I've outlined in this book) should be a means to an end — an opportunity to help more people and do more good in the world — not an end, in and of itself. Does being "sought-after" make you a "hot shot" in certain circles? Sure. Are some people who I consider to be highly sought-after literally "rich and famous?" Yes. But the people who are truly trusted and in-demand are also authentic; their fame and success is not their identity. And neither are the mistakes they made in the past.

Everyone has cringe-worthy workplace moments in their past. What becomes critical with so-called career-ending moves (CEMs) is whether you can make a mindset shift to survive them and move past them. Sadly, not everyone does; I've seen careers crash and burn in an instant. Our culture — in the United States and beyond — can be unforgiving. Sometimes it's just easier to show someone the door and forget they ever existed, and these "you're dead to me" decisions can happen at the drop of a hat or from a single misstep. You know, "the larger they are, the harder they fall," so to speak. But it takes courage to forgive ourselves, to reflect and learn, and move forward. And it takes courage to offer grace to a colleague or peer when they're mired in a difficult moment as well. Ed Staub, a wildly successful sales-training expert, told me: "The only reason to look back is to learn a lesson."

The bigger the CEM, the stronger you need to be if you're going to reflect and grow in the aftermath. For the purposes of your career, I challenge you to look at a CEM through a different lens. I'm going to challenge you to take that CEM and completely reframe the scenario. You cannot change the event (the past is the past), but you *can* change the long-term outcome of the event (the past is prologue). Now, you may need to spend some time licking your wounds — there are steps you will go through to process a legitimate career-ending move, as there is with any major life event. But let me ask you this: What do you do next? Can you see with fresh eyes a situation that appears, on the surface, to have *ended* whatever you had going for you and instead have it *define* — in a positive, even freeing, way — what you'll do next? Do you have the tenacity and patience to learn, reframe, and redefine?

The bigger the CEM, the stronger you need to be if you're going to reflect and grow in the aftermath.

I feel so strongly about this challenge that I'm changing the reference from CEM to "CDM" — Career-Defining Moments! For some people, they may remain CEMs. Only *you* control that mindset. So, the question is: Are you with me? Are *you* going to reframe your career bloopers from CEMs to CDMs? Are you willing and able to stop beating yourself up (and/or stop seeing other players in that big, ugly ordeal as the villains) so you can make space to ask yourself, "What big opportunity is this crisis creating for me?"

A CDM may stall your career at one company, but it can still serve to move your *career* forward. As one lily pad sinks, jump to another. I've often heard people use the phrase "make the leap" when talking about career moves, and it's not lost on me that sometimes our leaps result from being pushed (a little or a lot). Even when we're shown the door, we step into a world brimming with options and opportunities. Ironic as it might sound, had it not been for some of the idiotic things I have done (professionally, of course), I would not be sought-after today. Much of what has made me better has been the *result* of overcoming these mistakes.

I've often heard people use the phrase "make the leap" when talking about career moves, and it's not lost on me that sometimes our leaps result from being pushed (a little or a lot).

Let me share one last, dramatic story about workplace mistakes and career-defining moments. This next story is a doozy ... and sharing it publicly always makes me a little woozy. While I have told you that I am beginning to prefer the term "career-defining moments" instead of "career-ending moves," this story will demonstrate a legitimate *end* to a career with a company. Sometimes, a decision — a conscious behavior, a visceral blurt, the wrong facial expression or word choice — is so unforgettable to the people around you that it will forever color your reputation at that organization. The proverbial nail in my coffin at International Paper Company — the company from which I eventually leapt to establish my own company, HR Resolutions — took nearly a year to be hammered in ... but the coffin was constructed with one very memorable misstep in how I handled the almost impossible task of reporting to three bosses. Boy, talk about karma ...

The one *distinct* event that I can identify as a true and legitimate career ender was during my final year in an 8+ year tenure with International Paper Company. I was "a multi-facility human resource generalist" and I had the unenviable responsibility of reporting to three bosses: two regional vice presidents and one corporate HR director. It was more political than politics. I was young and had a big job — shouldering a great deal of responsibility for human-resources activities at seven facilities, in four states, across two unions, and with more than 500 employees. This position was the result of my third promotion with the company. All three of my bosses had *BIG EGOS*. (That's the nice way of putting it.) This was my first position where senior leaders — people of true corporate power — were to involve me in people decisions, such as terminations. I was being "sought after" for big, important conversations. It was an honor and a burden, all at once.

One day, there was a phone call. (Ugh, I remember this call like it just happened yesterday ... Some traumas never fade.) "Hello?" It was the vice president covering the New York market — big sales, big market, big opportunities. The CFO was also on the call. We were discussing an employee in his late 50s/early 60s who had enjoyed a long tenure with the company — an employee for whom there was no written documentation, coaching, counseling, performance reviews, or anything else in his file that would lead anyone to believe he was an underperformer. (Granted, his sales performance numbers were historically poor, and he *was* an underperformer, but no one wanted to hurt his feelings and tell him so.)

The VP was insistent — he *had* to fire this employee and the termination needed to happen *that day.*

I said," No." (You read that right, friends. I said no to a VP. I did it. Because I'm a rule follower and, by golly, policy says ...)

I'm quite thankful there was no such thing as a video call back then. The VP launched into a tirade. I remember it all, and the worst part of it was the comment "You little people have no idea" ... and on and on and on. Somehow, the call ended. His next call and my next call were both to my HR supervisor, Harry. My supervisor sent me home for the rest of the day because I was (almost) hysterical about the way the VP treated me. We all needed a "time out."

Harry also let me know that he told the VP to "do what he needed to do for the sake of the business" and that we would discuss that another time. I presumed that meant the VP was going to fire the employee who had been given no indication that he was on thin ice. And with no paper trail on performance issues with this employee, I was imagining the future allegations of "wrongful termination due to age." I wondered if the employee had a lawyer.

The following day, Harry (my supervisor) asked me to debrief him on that fateful and contentious call with the VP and the CFO. Harry asked me to explain what — exactly — went wrong with the conversation. I immediately started in on the facts that mattered to me as a human-resources professional: no documentation, no conversations, age protected, and on and on ... citing chapter and verse of our policies.

Harry then asked me to consider the fact that — even in the face of big issues and thoughtful, important, and even legal constraints and policies — HR professionals always have options, and we can also be diplomatic in responding to our superiors during crucial conversations. He told me that there are ways to speak and act that could allow HR professionals (like me and him) to maintain our good names and good standing as trusted advisors ... while still accomplishing our responsibilities of advocating for employees and minimizing the organization's risk.

While I was licking my wounds after the verbal tussle and the "you little people ..." dressing down from the VP, Harry had stepped in to handle the crisis. Harry then took the time to walk me through the conversation he had with the VP. In essence, Harry's messages to the VP who was on the verge of firing the employee "today!" boiled down to this:

1. **Why now?** What's so imperative that it must happen right now? What are the risks and benefits of an immediate termination?

2. **What came before this moment?** What informal discussions, if any, have you or others had with this salesperson about his performance?

3. **What are the other facts in this case?** What other data can you share with me so I can help you make this happen? (Customer complaints? Co-worker complaints? Insubordination? What's the "rest of the story?")

4. **OK. Here are your options.**

    a. Terminate today — Probably get sued

    b. Create and communicate a short-term performance-improvement plan (PIP) — Still risky for a lawsuit because he had such a long tenure with no indications of unacceptable performance

    c. Create and communicate a longer-term PIP — Lowest risk

5. **How do *you* want to move forward?**

6. **How can we *assist* you in moving forward?**

Huh. When it was all laid out for me in that calm, thoughtful way, I could see how an HR leader can (and should) play the role of trusted advisor in such situations — not as decision-maker with a "yes" or "no" verdict. Ultimately, the decision belonged to the vice president whose region the low-performing employee served. As a result of the conversation Harry had with the VP (as opposed to the kind of conversation I had with him), there was collaboration instead of conflict. By approaching such a situation with a "Here are the options as I see them ... Now, how can I help you?" mindset, my supervisor allowed the VP to do what he needed to do while HR did what they needed to do: Protect the company *and* be of service to our internal customers.

Pro Tip:
In almost any professional situation, you
can choose collaboration instead of conflict.
Think about the trusted advisors in your world — the people who are eagerly "sought-after" for their service and expertise. Take a moment to note how they embrace a collaborative mindset and how their reputations might be tarnished if they were confrontational in any way. Nobody wants to work with someone who is too rigid, "just the facts," and prone to right-fighting. It's possible to be right about your recommendations and still be in the wrong with how you behave. Becoming "sought-after" is, in many ways, about how you communicate and how you carry yourself.

Although the VP got to do what he needed to do for the business (he did, in fact, fire the salesperson that day), I wasn't forgiven for my transgressions. I was never promoted again. In fact, my career came to a screeching halt. I didn't just keep my head down and accept my fate — I did try to earn a promotion and find myself in the good graces of the C-suite again. I was battered and bruised, but I was not down and out. I had hope (at least for a little while). The next promotion I sought was in my hometown; the branch needed their own HR director. OMG — a chance for me to come off the road (I had been constantly on the road between our seven facilities across four states) but to stay with my current employer and get another promotion! Right?! It was perfect. I was perfect. The universe was serving up good things to me ...

Are you ready for a plot twist? Guess who the hiring manager was for the position? Yep — Mr. "You Little People" ... the VP to whom I had said "no." {Heavy sigh.} It was a dead end because of our history. My career-defining moment was clearly going to be my first career-ending move. I had no choice but to bide my time on the road.

Looking back on it all, I have more than an ounce of gratitude for what Harry taught me about diplomacy, communication, and balanced outcomes. Because the truth of the matter is that if I had never butted heads with a VP (and, by extension, the CFO) regarding that salesperson's termination decision, I may *never* have learned the lessons I did from that experience. (And there may never have been an HR Resolutions! Or this book you're reading right now.)

A Powerful Formula for Success

All these years later, I am still benefiting from and acting upon the coaching I got from Harry about how to lay out clear options and then let the right person make their own decisions within the contexts you have provided. This may be the one single area that I have applied to the remainder of my HR career. It is not my job to make the decision for my customer (or my internal customer if I'm an HR leader in a specific organization.) It *is* my job, however, to demonstrate my understanding of:

→ **My area of expertise** — Why they are reaching out to me for assistance

→ **The needs of the business** — What they need to accomplish

→ **The appropriate way to communicate to be heard** — How I am speaking to my audience

→ **The ability to be adaptable** — Options, options, options

In other words, it's vital to know *your* stuff, to know *their* stuff, to know the *audience*, and to be *flexible*. In a high-stakes situation or a problem-solving moment, if I have informed my customer of the risk involved and I have presented them viable options, I have done my job. I have demonstrated my understanding of their needs. I certainly don't have all the answers but, as a trusted advisor, it's my responsibility to look at all the pieces of the puzzle and come up with a solution (ideally, multiple solutions).

It's vital to know *your* stuff, to know *their* stuff, to know the *audience*, and to be *flexible*.

This is how I arrived at the premise for this book — the four building blocks for becoming sought-after:

➤ Know *your* stuff

➤ Know *their* stuff

➤ Know the *audience*

➤ Be *flexible.*

Think about it. Bring to mind anyone you look up to — someone you consider an "influencer" or an expert. Maybe you follow them on social media, have read their books, or would happily pay for a ticket to learn from them directly as a member of their audience. Whoever you have in mind started out by making mistakes. We were all beginners in the beginning. You are not alone on your journey — many people you admire have gone before you. And those who become sought-after have mastered the four building blocks. They have expertise (i.e., they know their own stuff); they understand the business contexts within which they or their stakeholders operate (i.e., they know other people's stuff); they communicate effectively and appropriately (or you wouldn't follow them, would you?); and they are flexible in their thinking and adaptive to change, time and time again.

Some Final Thoughts on Career-Defining Moments

Anytime you have a blooper, don't forget to take a few moments to "feel the feels." It's OK, really. If you don't move past the emotion of the situation, you will struggle to fully move on.

So, find a trusted colleague, peer, or mentor. Debrief the event with them — get a fresh set of eyes on the situation that aren't emotionally attached to it. Don't beat yourself up but *do* look at what honestly happened and what part you played in the story. Did you say "no" without asking for a clearer understanding? Did you react from the heart instead of the mind? Whatever the answer, I want to tell you: It's OK — we've all "been there and done that."

After you debrief what happened, re-examine the situation. What might you *do* differently in the future? How might you *react* differently if the same scenario arises again? Most importantly — what have you learned about *yourself*? What can you take away from the situation and make it "defining" and not "ending" for your job, career, or overall happiness?

Also, at end of the day — and you must trust me here — being terminated is *not* the end of the world. Anyone who lives and works long enough will be let go. It's practically inevitable. In fact, had I not been terminated in 2005, I would not be the owner of a successful boutique consulting firm, I would not be sought-after as a speaker, and I certainly wouldn't be a bestselling author. Not too shabby — even if I do say so myself — for someone who was fired for her "lack of people skills."

Seek to Understand: Homework Assignment #1

Learning from Your Career-Ending Moves, Bloopers, and Cringe-Worthy Mistakes

Take a few minutes to think about the moment you selected above — a point in your career when you said "hmmm ..." and realized you could have handled things differently and better. Use the space below to do some writing, or grab your favorite notebook or writing app.

Ask yourself:

- What was the situation?

- How did you respond at that time?

- How would you respond *today*?

- *Why* would you respond that way today?

_____

_____

_____

_____

What was your biggest learning opportunity through your own poor decision-making? Analyze the situation and explore what you learned (and when the lesson became truly clear and began benefitting you).

Where, when, and what was/were the defining moment(s) in your career? Describe your "before and after" personas.

_____

_____

_____

_____

CHAPTER 3

The Model

H R people (almost) always have the best interests of the company and the employees at the forefront of their minds. But (almost) always, HR people are viewed as the "no" department. *"If I go to HR, they're going to tell me I can't do this ... They're going to tell me I must document this ... They're just going to make my life harder."* Nobody wants to hear that kind of stuff (and HR people really don't want to be viewed that way!). Regardless of your profession, you probably have to say "no" from time to time (or a lot of the time!). Where are you saying "NO" to your audience? And are you saying it in a way that conveys confidence and respect? Or does every "no" chip away at important workplace relationships? Consider whether you can avoid saying "no" altogether and, instead, ask, "Have you thought about X, or Y, or Z?" Redirecting a line of thought instead of shutting it down is nearly always preferable. To be heard and be trusted, you have to demonstrate you have your audience's best interests in mind.

Where are you saying "NO" to your audience? And are you saying it in a way that conveys confidence and respect? Or does every "no" chip away at important workplace relationships?

At work and in life, it all comes down to the relationships. The only way to make a difference is to be trusted — to be listened to, to be "let in" to important conversations and decisions, to be respected for your perspectives and expertise, and to be recognized for your skills and insights. But how do you learn to do that? It's rare to find lessons for up-and-coming professionals on how to make a difference. There is no seminar or college class that is going to teach someone the skills necessary to be trusted. Yet trust is a competency that must be demonstrated in many positions. Imagine being a physician or nurse and not being trusted. Imagine working in human resources or the president's office and not being trusted. Imagine being an attorney or a salesperson, a highly paid consultant, a therapist, or a business coach and not being trusted. Being *sought-after* is another level of trust. I can trust any number of HR tacticians with confidential data, but I cannot trust them to advise me on effectively running a business. Sure, they can advise me on implementing policy and procedure, but running a business? Not typically. Sought-after professionals are those who can offer advice and change people's minds and perspectives. They can drive strategy. They can break down barriers and build bridges. Sought-after professionals are not just workplace "doers" — they are changemakers and sources of inspiration. No wonder so many of us want to be sought-after.

Becoming Sought-After, in Four Easy Steps — Guaranteed!

Well, OK. Maybe not guaranteed.

Let's talk about how to get from "here" to "there" in your career, and the steps many sought-after individuals have taken along the way.

If you're not a member of the C-suite, you probably don't lose sleep over the same things the C-suite does. And absolutely no one teaches us that (or talks about it much) when we're climbing the organizational ladder. It's no wonder front-line staff and even managers and directors (or other mid-level professionals in any industry) often feel like they're from Venus and their executives are from Mars; if our stressors and priorities are different, how can we ever be aligned? Listen up, friends: If you get nothing else out of this book, please work deliberately to learn what your executives and leaders are losing sleep over. Once they can see that *you* know what *they* care about deeply, then (and only then), they will seek you out for our expertise, your counsel, and your trusted involvement!

Lots of training can be found on communication styles; all types of assessments exist for individuals, leaders, and teams. You can learn how to *talk* to the team. But who teaches you how to be *heard* by the team? Perhaps you work in a profession where a string of initials behind your name (conveying academic or industry credentials) reinforces that you are a subject-matter expert (SME). And that's great — your credentials demonstrate an investment in your profession and continuing knowledge. But being educated or licensed or otherwise "credible" is not enough in the effort to become sought-after. Just because you have those initials does not ensure that anyone is going to *hear* what you have to say (or even come to the room where you're speaking). Education, credentialing, even experience — rarely is any of it enough to cause the leadership team (or other departments or enviable clients and audiences) to *seek* out your advice.

Hands down — being sought-after requires that you demonstrate:

1. **Professional Expertise** (know *your* stuff)

2. **Business Acumen** (know *their* stuff)

3. **Communications Expertise** (know the *audience*)

4. **Enthusiasm About Change** (be *flexible*)

This framework — in four interlocking steps or blocks — allows you to focus all your major efforts in your career ... as you seek to be heard, be trusted, and be recognized for your expertise.

As you have seen in Chapters 1 and 2, sometimes the best way to learn is through stories. So, I'm offering up several of them throughout the book. Each chapter will contain stories to illustrate or support the key arguments I make. Most of the stories will be about bloopers or career-defining moments — it seems I learn best that way! My hope is that the stories will help *you* see a situation and consider how it may compare to something in *your* professional past. You'll have the opportunity to ask yourself:

→   How might you have *felt*?

→   What might you have done *differently*?

→   How would you have *grown* from the scenario?

Apply my learnings (and missteps) to your own growth ... so you, too, can become "sought-after!" Guaranteed! (Or something like that.)

You may find you already have expertise in one building block — great! Take a moment to think about where you are in your career journey:

→   Perhaps you're new to a job in the banking industry (like being a mortgage underwriter), but you've worked in banking for more than a decade; that means you "know *their* stuff" (i.e., you understand the business), which will help you as you learn "*your* stuff" in your new area of responsibility.

→   Or maybe you're a subject-matter expert (like a digital marketing expert) but you just left the world of CPG (consumer packaged goods) and are now working in professional services; you've got building block #1 (subject-matter or functional expertise) locked and loaded, but you have a lot to learn about the business and the industry.

→   Or maybe you've got blocks #1 and 2 down pat (as a lot of leaders do), but you need help communicating more effectively (block #3) and/or you have a lot to learn when it comes to being adaptative and risk-tolerant in the face of change (block #4).

→   Block #4 — which requires that you be a champion for change — is difficult for almost everyone and can require constant work. Change is scary and unsettling; it's almost always easier to do things "the way we've always done them" than to step out onto the ledge of a new process, innovation, or way of thinking. But the truth of the matter is that people who were sought-after a decade ago but who haven't evolved their skills and their thinking will become dinosaurs in no time flat. It's not enough to *catch* up to your industry or profession's leaders of the pack — you have to *keep* up.

> **The truth of the matter is that people who were sought-after a decade ago but who haven't evolved their skills and their thinking will become dinosaurs in no time flat. It's not enough to *catch* up to your industry or profession's leaders of the pack — you have to *keep* up.**

Wherever you find yourself on the building-block structure, you can grow and improve. While reading this book, look for areas where you can focus on new learning that will enhance your professional growth; come back and read the area(s) you are already comfortable with after feeding on the "new" stuff. Feel free to jump around (in this book and in the work you're doing on yourself). There are no hard-and-fast rules about applying the building blocks in a specific order. In fact, there are elements you could probably apply tomorrow when you go into the office that will make a difference immediately. (So be sure to do that! Learn it today and use it tomorrow.)

Losing Sleep

Let's talk a little more about "losing sleep." I've seen the catch phrase in plenty of seminars trying to tell me what my CEO is losing sleep over. I always thought, frankly, it was a bunch of bull$#!% until I became a CEO who has lost sleep over so many things: payroll, client satisfaction, staffing, underperforming employees, increased costs of doing business, downturn in sales, upturn in sales (a good problem is still a problem!), and brand differentiation against the competition. It's amazing what a leader can lose sleep over. In fact — it's tiring just thinking about it — LOL!

Shame on me — I never once (before starting my own company) took the time to really *understand* what my boss was losing sleep over. I'll tell you what else is embarrassing ... I look back now and realize that I never even asked! I know what I *assumed* that my bosses and other superiors were losing sleep over: potential discrimination claims, implementing that new policy, where will we find enough employees, gee that contract costs a lot of money. Remember what happens when you assume? (If you're not sure, I'll let you look it up — I'm trying to keep the language clean.) **Go ask — right now ...**

> ### Shame on me — I never once (before starting my own company) took the time to really *understand* what my boss was losing sleep over. I'll tell you what else is embarrassing ... I look back now and realize that I never even asked!

Imagine how your CEO would respond if you presented them:

➜   Data relevant to *your* area of responsibility (e.g., marketing, sales, HR, finance, operations) *and* ...

➜   Its relevance to an area or issue *they* are concerned about ...

➜   In *their* communication style ...

➜   With a *plan* for implementation.

They will want more — they will begin to seek out your input, and eventually guidance, on that topic. Demonstrate your breadth of knowledge on a few more of the things the CEO is thinking about, when the time and moment is right. Don't get carried away — keep it within your area of expertise. Can you hear their sigh of relief? It *will* make a difference.

Having said that, you shouldn't lose sight of the things *you* are losing sleep over. You still have a policy to issue or capital expenditures to fund or a negative post on Facebook to address — those responsibilities never go away.

Managers, Leaders, and Trusted Advisors: Different But Alike

Manager, leader, trusted advisor. How do you define the differences between these three types of contributors to organizations and industries? What similar characteristics and traits flow between the three levels? Can a manager take a leap all the way to trusted advisor? How and why (or why not)? Does a leader — including someone who oversees and inspires a lot of managers — need to be a manager themselves, at least every now and again? Of course! Does a trusted advisor have to have come up through the ranks as a manager and/or leader? Why or why not?

The world of work has — for better or for worse — been a place ruled by hierarchies. Think about the kinds of words we use to describe our organizational charts and cultures: climbing the corporate ladder, "higher ups," bureaucracies, promotions and demotions, assistant and associate, junior and senior, superiors and subordinates, insubordination, staff and executives, and on and on. (And that's just in the civilian world. The military culture has even more formal and iron-clad ranks.) From our very first jobs in any type of organization or industry, we're familiarized with what it means to be "way up there" versus being "at the bottom of the totem pole." And we are often led to believe that the only path to the top — to the C-suite or to an enviable position as a sought-after celebrity/influencer/consultant — is by "paying our dues" at every rung of the proverbial ladder. While that's the path for some, it's not always necessary to bide your time for years on end at levels where you're not able to make your best contributions to the organizations and initiatives that need you.

As luck would have it, not everyone who is sought-after inside of an organization must be a *manager* or official leader within their organization. Why not? Because when your contributions are heard, trusted, and respected, it doesn't matter what your title is or how long your tenure has been. Remember the building blocks of being sought-after:

1. **Be a subject-matter expert** (i.e., know *your* stuff)

2. **Know the business** (i.e., know *their* stuff)

3. **Be able to communicate to all key stakeholders** (i.e., know the *audience*)

4. **Drive change and adapt** (i.e., be *flexible*)

When your contributions are heard, trusted, and respected, it doesn't matter what your title is or how long your tenure has been.

Think of a manufacturing maintenance technician who has maintained the efficacy and efficiency of a machine since the day it was installed. That technician certainly knows the machine, understands its use, can communicate to their boss about the needs of the machine, and can implement the changes necessary to keep the machine useful in a changing environment. Wouldn't that person be sought-after by the manager of the maintenance department? I sure hope so!

Reflection Question

What example can you provide of someone who doesn't lead, per se (maybe they don't have direct reports and they don't have a fancy title or profit-and-loss responsibility), but who is someone you seek out, over and over, for their expertise? Take a moment to reflect upon what they have done to make themselves so respected and even indispensable to you.

This is an important concept to grasp. Regardless of your position or title, you *can* be sought-after for your input. A title is just that — a title. Don't get hung up on the small stuff. Look at the building blocks necessary for earning the respect, trust, and attention of others ... then focus on the area where you can grow. Work toward applying all four building blocks to a situation like a presentation, then analyze how the presentation went. What worked well? What should be tweaked? At what moments could you observe that people were truly listening to you, trusting you, and offering up their respect by their behaviors, questions, or body language?

You don't need to be in the C-suite to be sought-after (and, frankly, the C-Suite isn't all it's cracked up to be — there's a *lot* of pressure there!). But wherever you're headed — and whatever title someone might someday bestow upon you (or that you might bestow upon yourself as you build your own personal brand) — consider that the four-step framework might also have a fifth element that we could just call "repeat." Enjoying a continuous journey of learning means acknowledging that you don't know everything, that the world is constantly changing, and sometimes you must go back to the beginning.

You might be thinking, "Wait. What? I thought that once I mastered the four building blocks, I'd be sought-after — highly acclaimed, renowned, and all that jazz." Yes, but ... Knowing *your* stuff is not evergreen. If you were a trader back when everyone stood on the crowded floors of stock exchanges (i.e., the open pit), shouting and flashing hand signals, but you didn't want to learn how to do the job once online trading changed the industry, you might have gone from "sought-after" to obsolete. At every turn, experts in any area need to upskill and reskill to remain relevant.

And what about when the overall business changes? Last year, you might have sounded credible in the conference room when you were talking about your company's two signature products; but if those products have been reengineered and/or your company now offers several new projects or services, you're going to need to re-learn what matters to your colleagues and customers. Likewise, just about the time you master the communication style of your boss or other key people who you want to be seeking out your opinion (like clients and others), your boss is apt to retire, or it might be time to impress new audiences and new prospects.

There's a reason why the fourth building block of the Sought-After Framework is about being adaptable to change. Just when you've become *the* expert in a particular space, the space will change. The key is to find these changes exhilarating or at least challenging in a positive way. Being sought-after for more than just a moment means you must be a champion for change.

Being sought-after for more than just a moment means you must be a champion for change.

Let's Start Building!

OK, now that you understand how the sought-after model works and why it matters, it's time to show you *how* to implement it in your life and work. The four chapters that follow each go deep into the nuances of a particular building block. We'll discuss the competencies (i.e., the demonstrable skills) that best support success in that area. Near the end of the book, we'll take a look at all the recommended competencies in a holistic and memorable way and I'll leave you with some final tips that might improve the overall likelihood of you being sought-after by the people and organizations where you want to serve, contribute, and BE A BIG DEAL.

Let me offer one caveat: You likely cannot be a master of all four building blocks *all* the time. And that's OK. Perhaps one of the most important messages of this book is that self-awareness is a critical component in each of the Sought-After Building Blocks. Know where you are and where you need to go. Then keep working to earn the right to be heard, be respected, and recognized for your expertise and your unique vantage points.

In the end, mastery of the building blocks (i.e., knowing *your* stuff, knowing *their* stuff, knowing the *audience*, and being *flexible*) will put you in a whole new light with your "audience." That audience may be:

→   Your immediate supervisor

→   Your supervisor's supervisor

- The interviewer or recruiter for your new job

- Your customers, clients, collaborators, or business partners

- Your readers, viewers, or listeners (if you're an author, a YouTuber or actor, or a podcaster or television commentator)

- Your audience members when you step on a stage or your followers when you communicate on social media.

The list of people for whom you might someday be sought-after is endless.

How do *you* want to be sought-after, and by whom? This book is here to help you get there solidly!

So, let's dive in!

CHAPTER 4

BUILDING BLOCK #1: Know Your Stuff

The first of the four building blocks is the need to "know your stuff." To be sought-after, you must be ready and able to demonstrate broad knowledge and deep expertise in a specialty, profession, work function, or topic. I would never have been invited to the decision-making table (or even promoted) in my career as a corporate HR professional if I was not competent in human resources. It doesn't matter if it's a functional area, like HR, marketing, finance, operations, logistics, or machine operation — or an industry, like healthcare, manufacturing, higher education, restaurants, or travel — having general knowledge of the area (i.e., being competent) and being able to *do* the work (i.e., demonstrating competencies) is everything. You must know what you are talking about (and you typically need to be able to prove you can do the work) when you want to be heard, be trusted, and be recognized for your expertise.

> You must know what you are talking about (and you typically need to be able to prove you can do the work) when you want to be heard, be trusted, and be recognized for your expertise.

Getting there takes time, work, and patience … and we'll all make mistakes on the way there. Oh, the embarrassing moments of our youth! With the last promotion I received at International Paper Company, I became what they called a Multi-Facility Human Resource Generalist. The sales folks called us "those MF HR people!" But all salty nicknames aside, I was thrilled to be in this visible and important role. As far as I was concerned, I had "arrived." As I shared in Chapters 1 and 2, I reported to two vice presidents and an HR director. And if you've ever had "dotted line" reporting to multiple bosses, you know that having more than one "commander" is not easy. One of my responsibilities was to represent HR on the Mid-Atlantic Regional Management Team — to claim my coveted seat in our group's top leadership team! I was the only woman on this management team (circa 1994) but that's a different story for a different book. (There are a few good stories there as well, particularly ones involving my husband as the only male spouse at management-team outings.)

During these bi-monthly meetings, leaders in sales, operations, and logistics from the individual branches of our company would seek ways to improve the business and the bottom line. We were led by a senior vice president named Humphrey and my debut appearance at the recurring meeting was the first time the group had anyone representing HR at the table with them. Well, this kid (at age 32) *almost* blew it.

There's a mistake that new leaders may make — they think they must contribute to *every* topic on the agenda. I thought that because I was there in the room, it was my job to say something about everything we discussed. I hope that the preparation for leadership meetings is better for newbies at your organization, but for me — back in the day — no one really taught us how to *behave* once we got invited to crucial conversations, started collaborating with the executive team, or even got promoted to the leadership team. After several meetings with the regional management team, my HR boss, Harry, called me. Humphrey, the senior vice president who oversaw the regional management team meetings, had advised my boss that I was no longer welcome in these meetings.

Sad, disappointed, hurt, surprised, and probably a tad angry, I asked what I had done wrong. Apparently, I "over talked." I had been trying so hard to "contribute" that I didn't fully comprehend how precious the time is when assembling a large leadership team and I hadn't developed good instincts about what thoughts and ideas of mine deserved "airtime" in the meeting and what could be kept to myself as I listened, learned, and took notes. (Unfortunately, I can still demonstrate this "over-talking" weakness today if I am unsure or insecure in my environment. I try to be conscious of this risk. But like many people whose imposter syndrome never quite goes away, I sometimes fill the uncomfortable silences with chatter ... of varying levels of quality. Perhaps you can relate.) Humphrey told Harry that I had an opinion on every topic that was discussed — whether I fully understood the area or not. (I was thinking, *"Well, frankly, HR does impact each area of the business,"* but ... Yeah. I had over talked and overstepped.) The other managers in the group were made uncomfortable and VP Humphrey was tired of hearing HR try to contribute to every discussion topic in the meeting.

I didn't think it was appropriate to just accept this feedback, accept my fate as ousted from the meetings, and do nothing to try to make it right. So, I asked my boss: "How could I make this better? Would it be appropriate to apologize to VP Humphrey?" Following the coaching from my HR boss, Harry, I immediately reached out to VP Humphrey and scheduled a one-on-one, in-person meeting with him. Frankly, I believe he was surprised by the request. When scheduling the call, I let him know that I wanted to personally apologize for disrespecting him and the team.

When we met, I did exactly that. I sincerely apologized for my overzealousness and asked him if I could have a second chance with his mentoring. We agreed that I would come back to the meetings, but that before I would speak at these meetings, I had to count to 10: I needed to honestly assess whether what I had to say would:

a. Be valuable to the whole group (i.e., Was this the right venue for my comments?).

b. Make a difference (i.e., Were my contributions likely to help shape a decision that was being made during the meeting?).

c. Be coming from a place of insight and expertise (i.e., Did I know what I was talking about?).

If (and only if) there was an item of importance to one of the team members (rather than the entire team), I should discuss it with them during breaks. At the next group meeting, I also made it a point to apologize to my peers — privately — for overstepping my bounds. To make a long story short, I was welcomed back into the group and became a regular valuable contributor from that point on (until my position was eliminated a few years later).

Why does this matter to you? Because there's a fine line between "knowing your stuff" and "being a know-it-all."

Reflection Question

Imagine you had been in my shoes — called out for over-talking in meetings with peers and leaders — and you had been given a second chance to communicate more effectively and to learn the difference between having a valuable insight and having a personal opinion. What learning might you have gotten out of this scenario? And what moments in your own career come to mind when hearing my story? What lessons can you learn now ... even if your missteps and cringe-worthy moments were years or even decades ago? It's never too late to know better and do better.

Know Your Stuff ... But Don't Be a "Know-It-All!"

You have probably been exposed to leaders or other professionals in your life who *live* to let you know how smart they are and how they know more than anyone else in their area of expertise (and probably a few other areas too). You know what? They very well *may* be that smart, and I say, "Good for them!" I also say, "What a potentially unbearable person to be around."

People should not have to feel a sense of dread when faced with the need to ask a question of an expert. But dread is the prevailing emotion I feel if I know that my simple and important question might result in a lengthy and unnecessary lecture. ("Just the facts, ma'am! Just the facts!") When seeking out information, insights, or advice from an expert, we should be excited, eager, and happy to learn from someone who really "knows their stuff" and can teach us something new. Ideally, consulting with an expert should be a positive experience — leading up to *and* following the interaction. But self-proclaimed experts (i.e., those who overstate their expertise, bask a little too much in it, or want you to kiss the ring or genuflect with gratitude after they help you out) are a whole lot to cope with. As such, sometimes true experts are *not* "sought-after" because they're more trouble than they're worth. Now, for my own reasons, if I have no other resource, I *will* turn to the self-proclaimed expert. But I'll try everything else first, before opening a can of worms with an egomaniacal expert. (Thank you, Google, for providing a no-ego option for information! You sometimes save the day!)

Reflection Question

If you are *already* "know your stuff," do you sense people are comfortable coming to you for information, unique perspectives, and advice? What action can you take to ensure that people don't feel apprehensive about asking you a question? And if you're just starting out in your field or profession, what can you do to balance your confidence in your expertise and the humility required for being truly heard and trusted?

You will lose credibility faster than you can *say* "credibility" if you constantly speak — especially when no one asked for your input. Trust me: You don't need to know everything about *everything,* and you don't even need to know everything in your own *field.* (And even if you *do* know a whole lot, you don't have to always be trying to prove your worth or intelligence by talking a blue streak about all the things you know.) Don't worry — Someone will usually ask you for input if they believe you have something to contribute. If your participation is not valuable to the topic of discussion, perhaps silence is golden.

If your participation is not valuable to the topic of discussion, perhaps silence is golden.

Let's flip the script for a moment to think about what it feels like to be a customer who is getting more than they bargained for from an "expert." Imagine that you're on the phone with a customer-service representative at a company that sells a product you're interested in buying. They have answered all your questions about their latest must-have technology widget; they listened to you and helped you find the exact item you need to do exactly what you need it to do — make your life easier. They have "sold" you, and you are ready to move to the purchase. You're waiting for the person on the phone to ask for your credit card number.

Then, quite unexpectedly, they start talking to you about another unrelated product that they sell — the new self-sanitizing water bottle that "will keep you hydrated all day long!" Granted, staying hydrated is a good thing. But what does hydration have to do with your tech widget? And who asked the customer-service rep anyway? While they were eager to be helpful, and we can all appreciate that, you couldn't care less about what they have to say about water bottles. Your "trust" or confidence in their advice starts to wane. You may even think, "They don't care about me and my needs; they just want to sell me one more thing!"

Imagine that individual going on and on and on (but never getting your credit card number and placing the order for the product you wanted). Their behavior might have changed your overall opinion of the company. And you might hang up and go buy your tech widget from someone else. I am almost physically shuddering as I write this, because my initial senior leadership team meetings are all replaying in my head. I was like that customer-service rep — I couldn't help but talk about *all* the things on my mind, even if it wasn't what my audience needed or wanted in that moment. I get it now — I didn't need to ask every question, share every story, or prove to my colleagues that I knew a little something (or *thought* I knew something!) about everything on the meeting agenda. I only needed to know about and contribute to the topics I was there for — HR. I needed to "stay in my lane." Trying to be a "know-it-all" damaged my credibility with my peers and with the leadership team.

Interestingly enough, I just Googled "know-it-all" and here are the synonyms, according to *Merriam-Webster*: [5]

➤   Smart Aleck

➤   Smarty-Pants

---

5   https://www.merriam-webster.com/thesaurus/know-it-all

➤ Wiseass

➤ Hot Shot

➤ Show-Off

➤ Wisecracker

I don't know about you, but these are not nicknames I want applied to me. And I can't imagine that I would often be prompted to seek out advice or guidance from someone with such a reputation. So, wherever you are in your career, while it's vital to continually learn and try new things, consider the fact that being curious and being a "know-it-all" are two different things. Curious professionals listen, study, read, and ask just the right number of questions — to the right people, at the right time. "Know-it-alls" talk, boast, assume, and dominate the conversation — without regard for the needs and expectations of their audience.

> **Curious professionals listen, study, read, and ask just the right number of questions — to the right people, at the right time. "Know-it-alls" talk, boast, assume, and dominate the conversation — without regard for the needs and expectations of their audience.**

Knowing Your Stuff: Why This Building Block Is Important

Part of "knowing your stuff" is the ability to *demonstrate* that you know your stuff (because if nobody *knows*, it's hard to *help* anybody at all). Demonstrating your expertise takes some *work* on your part. It also takes some *time*. As hard as it may be to hear, you won't be considered an expert in your field when you're fresh out of school or brand new to an industry. No matter how smart you are, "overnight success" never happens overnight. You must pay your dues. I know, I know — you're probably tired of hearing that, but these "dues" — in the end — give you the street cred of "knowing your stuff!" And without credibility, you'll never be sought-after. I have seen too many professionals get a year or two under their belt in a particular industry or profession, get promoted too quickly because they are good at selling themselves, and then implode just a few years later. Often, they stagnate and never truly reach the level of Subject-Matter Expert.

Demonstrating your expertise takes some work on your part. It also takes some *time*.

Being able to demonstrate your expertise requires you to walk the fine line between over-contributing and seeking out meaningful opportunities to contribute. You will be surprised where you can find these opportunities. A great way to gain expertise (and free leadership training) is through community service. There are a lot of added advantages here as well, not to mention the good will for your employer — they get some mileage out of your volunteer work as well.

Two of my earliest employers had a requirement that every employee participate in a voluntary capacity (I realize the irony here — *requiring* that people *volunteer*) in some type of community organization, such as Rotary, Kiwanis, Lions Club, or other local charities. At first, I always assumed this staff requirement was in place to enhance the good name of the company and provide a way to get the company's name "out there" for sales purposes. What you quickly learn in these charitable organizations, though, is "no selling!" While you are there *because* of your company, you are (or should be) there for the good of the community. Giving a sales pitch for your business while working at a charity auction or donating your time to the local Boys and Girls Club is bad form. And, as it turns out, just being there is "good PR." It's funny, but I have noticed that the less you talked about business when volunteering in the community, the more business you got — it was all about building credibility and trust!

These organizations (most of which are non-profit and mission-driven) all have committees and leadership opportunities. Once in leadership with the organization, you will most likely be required to take their leadership training. You will also be exposed to diverse ideas, people, and perspectives through these organizations. Even if you don't follow any of their leadership paths, you will still have a group of trusted advisors who you can turn to for guidance and mentorship. Thirty plus years later, I still have trusted colleagues from my first outing as a Kiwanis member. People who volunteer together "stay together."

So, go ahead — share your knowledge ... at work and through your volunteer activities. Bit by bit, your expertise will become known among people who might someday truly need you, appreciate you, listen to you, respect you, and help you grow. Knowing your stuff and demonstrating, *appropriately,* is Building Block #1 in becoming sought-after. And remember: There's no need to show-off! You are in this space at this time for a reason — you've earned the opportunity and the *right* to contribute.

"Know Your Stuff" Competencies

Let's get down to brass tacks. At every stage of becoming sought-after, there are things you must be able to *do* — competencies you must demonstrate, consistently and to a high standard. Nobody who ever makes it to the pinnacle of their profession does so by just talking a good game or being full of theory without action. While many sought-after experts do, of course, eventually earn the right to talk about, analyze, teach, strategize, and consult on things they no longer need to handle from a tactical standpoint (e.g., a pediatric heart surgeon might no longer be operating on patients but might be considered a leading authority on their specialty), we all start out as "doers" before we earn the right to be leaders, commentators, or experts.

So, what must you do to prove that you "know your stuff?" Who must you be, and what character traits must you demonstrate, every day and in every possible way?

Experts who "know their stuff" are:

- ➜ Vulnerable

- ➜ Confident

- ➜ Humble

- ➜ Curious

Let's explore these traits and values — these competencies of subject-matter expertise, regardless of your profession.

Vulnerability

There will be naysayers. There always are. You will be challenged. Someone will believe they know more than you (and they might) *or* someone will try to show others that you don't know all that you profess to know. The worst are the folks who are fully aware that they don't know what they're talking about but who don't want you to get all the attention — the limelight, respect, or even adoration. My mom always told me those people were just jealous! And, certainly, some of them are. If you're the person in the room who is regarded as a leading authority or the resident expert, others who wish to be similarly regarded might feel threatened — especially in a corporate culture where pecking order matters and where we all want to be "the golden child" in the eyes of the leadership team.

So, whether you're already considered an expert (who "knows their stuff") or you're on your way to achieving such a status, it's important to be vulnerable. It's especially important to be vulnerable when being challenged or even attacked. Maybe your peers are playing devil's advocate with you and you're feeling disrespected. Or maybe someone keeps cutting you off when you're talking or is dismissive of your ideas (even though you know your ideas have merit). Don't get defensive ... get vulnerable.

Don't get defensive ... get vulnerable.

Many people make the mistake of thinking vulnerability is the act of rolling over and admitting defeat — of being someone's doormat or punching bag. But that's not what workplace or career vulnerability is about. Being vulnerable does not make you a victim; it makes you approachable, human, measured, kind. Think about people who can say, "Yes, you're right. Your idea is an excellent one and even better than the one I just proposed." Or "I apologize. While I know a lot about this topic, I don't know everything. And I got this one wrong. Thanks for fact-checking me here." This kind of vulnerability doesn't make someone fall from grace as the sought-after expert you've always regarded them as; in fact, vulnerable experts reinforce their expertise through these moments of admitting their shortcomings and highlighting their humanity. Sometimes, "I don't know" is the right answer. And sometimes "I'm sorry" elevates you more than it diminishes you.

Sometimes, "I don't know" is the right answer. And sometimes "I'm sorry" elevates you more than it diminishes you.

On your journey to learn everything you can about your chosen area of expertise, you will be challenged and questioned. Challenges are OK. Handle them with a calm, vulnerable demeanor, and approach them honestly. When you do this, the challenges you face can reinforce your standing as a reliable source of information on your team, in your company, or even across your industry. Begin to think of vulnerability as a tool that you can use when demonstrating your knowledge and expertise. Stay strong, but always be willing to listen to differing opinions. Indeed, there is always more to learn and you're not always the only (or smartest) expert in the room.

Another important element of vulnerability is being able to handle constructive criticism. Nobody starts their day thinking: *"Boy, I hope someone has constructive criticism for me today!"* But if no one ever cares enough about us to take the time to provide actionable feedback, how will we ever "course correct" if we veer a bit from the charted path in our professional behaviors? I won't lie — constructive criticism can *hurt*. Making mistakes (and getting called out for them) sucks! I am right there with you; like most people, I tend to take things very personally. As a result, I often fall into the trap of feeling deflated and even defeated — at first — when constructive criticism comes my way. It's far too easy to think that constructive criticism isn't just about the *work* product, but that it's about *me*! One way I deal with the emotion of vulnerability is to allow myself the *time* to be embarrassed, sad, disappointed — all the "feels" that go along with criticism. But the time is measured — I put an end time on it. I let myself be bummed for a few minutes or a few hours (and in the case of big feedback, maybe a few days). Basically, I tell myself: *"OK, you screwed up ... Take the time to chew on it, then get over it!"*

There is a second, very important component to the "get over it" phrase. I don't think we should ever allow ourselves to "get over it" (or to sweep it under the rug) without taking the time to learn from the feedback and make decisions or develop strategies to ensure that the mistake won't be repeated and/or that our stakeholders won't ever need to deliver that same "constructive criticism" again. Ask yourself: "What did I *learn* and what can I *do* so this won't happen again?" I also strongly encourage my staff to approach their mistakes this way. I don't want them beating themselves up over mistakes that don't define them and that can teach them something important. This is a critical, secondary piece of vulnerability — the learning piece. Own your mistakes — learn from them — move on. It *is* OK ... I promise!

Confidence

To demonstrate you "know your stuff," you must first have trust in yourself. The surest path to becoming an expert who has impact on the world involves first believing in the power and importance of what you have learned, researched, experienced, and discovered along your way. Alongside the vulnerability that is a vital competency of "knowing your stuff" or being a subject-matter expert is a healthy dose of confidence. And confidence can be demonstrated in a lot of different ways. Sometimes *being silent* demonstrates a level of confidence in your surroundings or your team. Sometimes *speaking up* demonstrates confidence in your knowledge about a situation. A wise leader knows when a situation calls for either … or both.

The surest path to becoming an expert who has impact on the world involves first believing in the power and importance of what you have learned, researched, experienced, and discovered along your way.

Another important part of confidence is your body language and how you carry yourself. Just before I go on stage for speaking engagements, I do a "superhero pose" to psyche myself up (remember imposter syndrome from early on …). I will be honest — I learned about this on *Grey's Anatomy* when neurosurgeon Dr. Amelia Sheppard started doing this before every high-stakes surgery, putting herself in the right frame of mind to do superhuman work. Many of you might have first learned about the power of confident body language from the groundbreaking TED Talk by Amy Cuddy, "Your Body Language May Shape Who You Are." And standing with your feet far apart, your chest out and your face up, and your hands on your hips really can work — it puts me in the right mental place to be confident in what I'm presenting. It also helps improve my posture by pushing my shoulders back (and belly in — LOL!). When I walk on stage, I am confident that I am ready to go! I know my stuff, and I'm ready to share it with others.

I will let you in on a little secret here. (See? Vulnerability.) On a personal basis, I am incredibly shy. I suffer from Social Anxiety Disorder and, if I'm not careful, it can eat into my confidence at any moment. In a business setting, it's completely the opposite. I "own" the room … when I'm playing the role or persona of "Karen, Businesswoman." Technically, I'm an ambivert — I have traits and characteristics of *both* an extrovert and an introvert, depending upon the situation. You know what else? I'm not embarrassed by that — recognizing that it's a persona (that I can put on and take off, like a fancy outfit) is what gets me through and provides me the self-confidence to do what I do professionally. It's not that my work-place persona isn't authentic — it's all me. But it doesn't come naturally or easily. If you, too, are shy or introverted, I encourage you to try this approach: Examine your "work" persona and determine if that helps bring you out of your shell while adding some self-confidence to your toolkit.

Humility

Remember the discussion we had about "don't be a know-it-all?" Sometimes that requires being humble and acknowledging that we simply do *not* know it all. Humility is a powerful tool for sought-after experts, and it's not counter-intuitive to confidence. You can be truly confident about your areas of expertise and still be humble about it. If you want people (e.g., audiences, clients, coworkers, other stakeholders) to listen to you, trust you, and respect and recognize you for your expertise, you must first approach every interaction and relationship in the spirit of being courte-ously respectful.

You can be truly confident about your areas of expertise and still be humble about it.

Paired with vulnerability and confidence, humility is a key character-istic necessary to clearly demonstrate mastery of the "Know Your Stuff" building block. There is no need to be overtly boastful when you are confident in your field. Sure, you need to demonstrate your knowledge, your sharp thinking, your wise decision-making — especially in the early years of your career. But once you are recognized as someone who has mastered the first building block — once you are regarded as someone who "really knows their stuff," you won't need to *keep* proving your ability to be sought-after. When seeking to be visible to new audiences (new prospective clients, new bosses, new business partners, etc.), even the most credible experts have to start from zero in communicating their expertise. Personal branding and some savvy skills in being visible and even "tooting your own horn" will always be necessary from time to time.

But true experts always balance their confidence with humility, learning to say, "Yes, I wrote a book on that topic; I'm so glad *you* found it useful. Tell me more about *your* work!" (And yes, one of the easiest ways to stave off the need for boasting is to have social proof of your functional, topical, or industry expertise.) If you've "written the book on it," have been featured in authoritative media outlets, or have had others singing your praises online and at work, you don't have to work so hard at proving your expertise — and risk coming off as egotistical. If everyone else thinks you're pretty amazing, you rarely need to remind them.

It's not easy. These character traits and behaviors are often at odds with one another. How can you be confident (and curious!) while also being vulnerable and humble? Sometimes you'll find the perfect balance, and other times, you won't. But mastering these competencies and living by them can go a long way toward helping you become sought-after in your field. You need to be confident, respectful of others (leadership, your team), *and* you need to be humble. Stir it up just right and people will seek you out for your opinion and expertise!

Curiosity

Let's explore the fourth critical competency of being able to demonstrate that you "know your stuff." You might have noticed that I dropped the word "curious" into the paragraph above. That's because curiosity is the final competency required for building block #1, Knowing Your Stuff. Some people think of curiosity as a commitment to "continuous learning." Whatever you call it, it matters.

Your field is changing and progressing. Every moment. Now, unless you are the researcher, scientist, or developer who is *creating* all the change, you aren't going to know everything about your field. To demonstrate you Know Your Stuff, you must constantly be learning. You need to show that you keep up with the latest trends, ideally in both your *profession* (e.g., pediatrics, accounting, marketing, human resources) and your *industry* (e.g., clinical healthcare, manufacturing, higher education, banking). More about that later.

Look at the human resources profession — goodness, I think it changes almost overnight, practically *every* night. There is no possible way I can know everything there is to know about human resources because of the constantly changing legal requirements, rules and regulations mandated by governmental bodies, and societal trends. I acknowledge that when someone asks me a question that I don't know the answer to, I prefer to answer: "I'm not sure but let me find out!" (If you do the same thing, it's vital that you then make sure to follow up after finding out!)

The options for continuous learning are endless. Heck, I'm sitting in a library writing right now, surrounded by books and journals and computer databases — what a great treasure-trove of resources! The following are some tips on where and how to satisfy your curiosity, so you can achieve and maintain subject-matter expertise through continuous learning.

What if I'm "Weak" Here? — Practical Tips for Brushing Up Your "Know Your Stuff" Competencies

Places to Turn:

➜ **Professional associations:** What organizations represent people like you? Can you attend their conferences or seek mentorship or access timely content on their websites?

➜ **Professional certifications:** Some professions require continuing education to maintain status or licensure, so turning to courses or certifications can keep you sharp *and* help you check off a job requirement.

➜ **Professional newsletters/magazines/podcasts/webinars:** The formal learning opportunities are myriad. And they're often free!

Practices to Put in Place:

➜ **Ask a trusted colleague for feedback and input** about your work (in general and regarding drafts of presentations, reports, articles, or other high-stakes work).

- **Have a one-on-one with your naysayer(s).** Learn to confront criticism in real time, with an open mind and a lot of vulnerability and humility. Rather than run from tension or conflict, lean in.
- **Make a concerted effort to close the loop.** After important interactions, projects, or conversations where something goes sideways, endeavor to always "debrief" — either by yourself or with a mentor. The immediate moments following a mistake are amazing opportunities to learn and grow.

Curious Behaviors to Embrace:

- **Listen to learn.** *Ask* questions before *answering* questions.
- **Go deep.** Seek clarity any time you have even 5% of a knowledge gap or a moment of "I wonder ..."
- **Model the behavior you see.** Have a conversation with someone *you* believe to be the humblest when it comes to their expertise, intelligence, or practical experience in your area. Find out how to be more like *them* as you seek to be the best version of *you*.

Seek to Understand: Homework Assignment #2

Becoming a Subject-Matter Expert with Admirable Attitudes and Behaviors

Exercise #1: Accepting Feedback

Describe a specific time when you received constructive criticism. Begin with setting the stage for exactly what prompted the feedback.

a.   Who provided the criticism? _____

b.   How did you feel? _____

c.   Was the criticism fair or justified? _____

d.   How did you respond? _____

e.   What did you do with the information? _____

f.   Have any similar situations arisen? If so, what did you do differently (if anything) after this memorable moment in accepting constructive feedback? _____

Exercise #2: Confront the "Ego" in Expertise

Think of a colleague who is, by all accounts, a "know-it-all." How do you respond to them? How do others respond to them? Do you sense they are competent and confident? Could they be insecure or uncomfortable? How might you be able to help them?

_____

_____

_____

_____

Exercise #3: "Know Your Stuff" Self-Assessment

Rank yourself in each competency: Vulnerability, Confidence, Humility, and Curiosity

a. Which is your strongest? How do you demonstrate the competency daily?

_____

_____

_____

b. Which is your weakest? How have you demonstrated this on occasion?

_____

_____

_____

c. What actions will you take to leverage the opportunities of your strongest area and to improve your abilities in your weakest area?

_____

_____

_____

CHAPTER FIVE

BUILDING BLOCK #2:
Know Their Stuff

N ow that you know a whole lot about mastering Building Block #1, "Know Your Stuff," let's advance to Building Block #2 — "Know *Their* Stuff." And I don't just mean "know the financials," blah, blah, blah. I'm talking about the importance of really knowing the business (and the overall industry or competitive environment) in which your subject-matter expertise must fit. To be sought-after, you must be ready and able to demonstrate knowledge and a level of expertise in the business you are supporting. Using human resources as an example, if I attempt to lead in an HR role but don't have a solid understanding of how the overall business works, I'll never fully understand how my recommendations and guidance will impact the operation. And, at end of the day, it's the operation (and the people who power that operation) that creates the need for human resources in the first place.

Remember earlier when I talked about NAFTA and the impact to the steel plant where I worked? Another career learning moment came with this event. I had forgotten about the needs of the operation when it came time to determine which employees were going to be laid off. It's never easy to balance continuing production demands while eliminating segments of a workforce. Ultimately (even when times are tough and dollars are short), the product still needs to be manufactured. In the case of the company that I was working for, the Union Contract stipulated "last in, first out." That meant that the newest employees were to be the first to be cut in the event of a layoff. Well, not all the senior people — the people who had been there for a long time — had all the skills necessary for the remaining jobs. I disregarded the needs of the business and plowed ahead with the black-and-white details of the contract. Last in, first out.

Thankfully, production did *not* come to a screeching halt ... but my actions made the work itself and the scheduling of employees across the various shifts significantly more difficult. In that one moment, I lost the trust and confidence of the operations leadership. I made their jobs harder. I forgot the needs of the business.

Reflection Question

When have you made someone's job more difficult? How could a better understanding of the overall business have prevented that misstep? And what can you do — for yourself and for the people who report to you — to ensure you minimize the chance of creating friction or pain for others by first maximizing your understanding of the business? Take a moment to think about your "Know Their Stuff" successes and failures.

When it comes to "knowing their stuff" and learning about the business, luckily, not all lessons are negative. When I was first promoted to assistant personnel manager and started having responsibility for recruiting warehouse personnel, I asked the vice president of operations to let me work a shift in the warehouse so I could learn how to load a truck. Now, Jerry looked at me like I had three heads and, initially, said no. He insisted it was not my place. I persisted. He relented (I can be a nuisance!) and I worked a 2nd shift, on the floor, picking product, arranging pallets, and loading trucks. It was hard work (and I am a disaster when trying to operate a forklift). I was probably more distraction than help, but I learned a great deal ... which, ultimately, helped me understand better how to hire personnel for the warehouse. (I knew not to hire people like me!)

I'm hopeful that this story has you thinking about ways in which you have shadowed people in other areas of your business, or that it's got you planning such an experience for the future. If you've ever seen the television show *Undercover Boss*, you have a sense of why this is important. Why do you think I did this exercise as a not-so-undercover HR manager, trying her hand at a role she needed to better understand? What do you think came out of this venture onto 2nd shift in the warehouse? The results were powerful:

1. I learned how difficult the work is (8+ hours standing on a concrete floor). That understanding led to greater respect.

2. I was able to speak, firsthand, about the job to candidates for positions in the warehouse. My improved perspective (and respect for the people in those roles!) allowed me to make better matches during the hiring process.

3. Operations supervisors and personnel learned to trust my recommendations because I had worked — albeit just for a single shift— side-by-side with them. Mutual trust made future communications and collaborations easier and more efficient.

Getting up close and personal with workers in all areas of our operations became increasingly important to me. After that first experience in the warehouse, I sought out more opportunities to learn. I rode with drivers to deliver product; I sat with customer service employees, taking phone call after phone call; and I rode with sales personnel to new and existing account visits. It made a difference — for my "customer" (the employees) and for my understanding of how my work impacted their work. I demonstrated to my coworkers that I wanted to understand *their* perspective on the work. Knowing *their* business matters.

Knowing Their Stuff: Why This Building Block Is Important

Understanding the "business" of your business is an important skill for anyone seeking to be sought-after. Simply stated, you need to understand the answers to these critical questions:

- How does our company make money?

- What are our products and services?

- What makes us different from our competitors?

➥   Who are the customers?

➥   Where do we find and engage our customers?

➥   How do we lose customers?

➥   Who are our partners and vendors, and how does our supply chain work?

➥   What are the biggest threats to our success?

➥   Where and how do we lose money/margin?

➥   How are we planning to grow, be more nimble, or offer something new?

You might be familiar with Dr. Stephen R. Covey's Fifth Habit — "Seek First to Understand, Then to Be Understood."[6] First understanding others (people, businesses, strategies) is critical as a building block to demonstrating your own expertise. "Knowing their stuff" in my sought-after model is quite similar to "seek first to understand" in Covey's habits framework. It comes back to having a thorough understanding of the operations of the business so *you* can give your best guidance when sought-after for your input, even in day-to-day questions. This building block applies in any function, responsibility, business type, or industry.

Ed Staub is one of the sought-after experts I interviewed while writing this book, and I asked him to reflect on this idea of "knowing their stuff," and he gave me a fresh perspective on how he applies the concept across industries and for people in various types of roles. As a life-long sales and culture trainer in the Sandler Training model, Staub often talks about workplace "pain" — suggesting that we have to "focus on their stuff, their pain" so we can match our stuff to their needs. Indeed. Sometimes the "stuff" of others is about what they worry about and what they dream about — about fears and pain, plus aspirations and goals. And these driving emotions (good and bad) are always tied to how the business (or a portion of the business, like a specific division, department, or team) runs. The better we understand the ins and outs of "their" business, the more value we can deliver.

---

6 https://www.franklincovey.com/habit-5/

So, ask yourself:

➤ How will *my* recommendation(s) impact *their* work?

➤ How will *my* recommendations get to the right prospective client base?

➤ How will *my* priorities translate to *their* realities? (How will enforcing this accounting standard, for example, impact the ability to introduce a new product line?)

"You need to know your audience if you're going to contribute to them. You have to know what they need. You have to know what they're going through," said Steve Gilliland, who so thoughtfully penned the foreword for this book and participated in an interview about what it takes to be "sought-after."

A Story for Learning:
How One Wrong Utterance Can Leave Them Thinking You Don't "Know Their Stuff"

During our chat about what it takes to be "sought-after," Kate Colbert shared the following story about how not "knowing their stuff" can end a business relationship before it even begins.

"When serving as the director of communications for a 100-year-old medical-sciences university, I was playing a key role in renaming and completely rebranding the institution for the future. To help us with this major initiative, we needed a partner. Several firms came to us with presentations — the proverbial dog-and-pony show in the board room, with our discerning president and the rest of the C-suite assembled, ready to be wowed. One firm, that I really wanted to work with and that had demonstrated expertise in higher education and even in healthcare (i.e., our two industries), brought a diverse group of talent to speak to the president and our committee. Prior to the meeting, if you had asked me to wager on which firm was going to win our business, I would have said this one.

They understood medical schools, health systems, and academia in general.

"To be fair, we were a little different from some colleges and universities in that we were a *graduate* school — we didn't offer bachelor's degrees, just MD, DPM, MS, DPT, and PhD credentials. I was confident they understood that our students were all working on advanced degrees and that you'd have to be a prodigy to enroll at our university much younger than 23. In normal meeting fashion, before jumping into the agency's presentation on how they could help us change our name and our reputation, we had everyone introduce themselves. Our internal team each said a few words, then the agency leaders introduced themselves. Their credentials and experiences were impressive.

"The very last person to introduce herself to the university leadership team was a young woman — perhaps just a few years into her career as a brand marketer. She was absolutely dressed the part and looked confident and prepared, with a leather padfolio on the table in front of her. She explained, clearly and with poise, where she earned her undergraduate degree and what her responsibilities were with the firm. The next words out of her mouth were her company's death-knell: 'I have expertise in understanding the attitudes and behaviors of the teen market.'

"No one asked her to elaborate, and we then sat through an impressive one-hour presentation with case studies from their other clients. They were a 'wow.' Their executives knew their stuff. But I could tell that our president thought this was a waste of his time. I was a bundle of nerves, as I was the communications director who assured my senior leaders that this company deserved to be considered for our monumental project. I couldn't figure out why the tension in the room was so thick you could have cut it with a knife. But I was about to find out.

"After we walked the agency team out the door, my colleagues and I got an earful from the president. 'Do they even know what we do here?!' he bellowed. 'The one girl was bragging about having a finger on the pulse of the teen market. We're a graduate school! We don't recruit teenagers!'

"Oh, boy. One little phrase had sunk them. Had this junior member of the agency team truly understood the business we were in — the business of educating graduate students for careers in clinical healthcare and biomedical research — she might have known that talking about teens (the customers that undergraduate universities are recruiting) was a misfit for us. She was sharp and she proved her value during the meeting, but the president wasn't listening to her at that point. In fact, he was barely listening to anyone; his mind was made up. There would have been numerous other ways for Miss Teen Spirit to discuss 'her stuff' — like her passion for market research and her experience planning big events and working with journalists — in a way that that would have related to 'our stuff.' But she'd blown it.

"While the rest of the agency's presentation was spot on (and it was clear in my mind that they would have been a worthy partner in our name-change initiative), I could not change the president's mind. The *only* thing he heard was, "I have a finger on the pulse of the teen market" and what he saw was a young professional — probably the same age as our students — who he didn't believe had earned the right to be in our board room. The agency couldn't have saved themselves if they'd tried. In the mind of our university's president, there was absolutely no way we were going to pay a lot of money to — and invest a lot of time, energy, and effort into a partnership with — somebody who doesn't understand the business we're in."

See? "Knowing their business" is important! (And I can't help but wonder if that young professional understood how one phrase from her resulted in her firm losing the bid for a huge piece of business.) The lesson is stark — when trying to serve someone (inside your own business or as a consultant or vendor), failure to understand what they do, who they serve, how they do it, and what they need can be a prelude to disaster.

"Know Their Stuff" Competencies

Being seen as someone who has a 30,000-foot view of the organization and even the entire industry allows you to be selected for important projects, responsibilities, presentations, and more. When you can show your colleagues or clients that you "know their stuff" in addition to knowing your own, you're a significant step closer to being trusted and respected. The three key competencies you should be able to demonstrate when seeking to "know their stuff: are:

- ➡ Business acumen

- ➡ Questioning

- ➡ Active listening

Business Acumen

First and foremost, you need to understand how businesses function, with particular insight about the type of business where you're seeking to be sought-after. There are many types of organizations: non-profit, for-profit, publicly held, privately held. They all operate a bit differently. If you want to be hired to speak at conferences in the interior design and architecture industries, then you need to understand how those types of businesses work. Or if you work inside a hospital, it would behoove you to understand how your role fits into the overall operation and how the hospital runs. Then, you need to dig into the specifics of your business audience — the "audience" you're trying to prove yourself to might be your boss, the C-suite, the board, or the founder. If you are an employee and are classified as "overhead" (like HR is), you may have a more difficult road to demonstrate your competency here because we are often the financial thorn in the side of operations personnel.

Again, you don't have to perfectly understand the financial statements (unless you work in accounting and finance!) but you *do* need to understand what makes the business tick. This leads into our next competency: Questioning.

Questioning

Be curious (but don't be nosy!). Learning about *their stuff* can automatically lead to questioning but let's address it now as an actual skill to be worked on and learned. It *can* be learned. I'm naturally curious (which, for me, means I'm always reading and seeking out information so I can know more, do more, and be more). But being curious — while it can help you go deeper into your own functional expertise (i.e., "know your stuff") isn't the same thing as knowing how to ask great questions to colleagues, clients, and partners. It's possible to be curious in a personal way but to go mute when faced with the opportunity to ask questions that would help you to better "know *their* stuff." I tend to forget to ask questions when working with others because I am so excited to address the problem. (See? We all need to be continuously learning and self-evaluating!)

According to Jim Rowell, co-author of the book *The 10 Keys to Effective Supervision: Building Healthy Cultures Through Servant Leadership*, questioning is one of the ways we demonstrate that we are of service to our audience. Imagine the scenario from Chapter 2 with the VP who insisted upon firing the poorly performing salesperson right then and there. I dug in my heels and said, "No," not realizing that my rigid adherence to HR rules might be a career-ending move for me. How else might that relationship have been different if I would have tried to see the situation through his eyes — if I had politely and calmly asked him to help me understand why he wanted to move forward with the termination so quickly? And what might have happened, during yet another career-defining moment, if I had consulted (i.e., truly *listened* to) the operations team when I had to direct the layoffs in the steel plant?

The first step to asking good questions is slowing down! Unless the situation is an actual emergency, you have time. Remind yourself that "knowing their stuff" involves an investment in learning as much as possible about the situation. Most times, when communicating and contributing outside your immediate field, you will only accomplish the goal of learning a great deal by asking questions. My favorite phrase — "Help me understand" — truly opens the conversation. Everyone wants to be understood. You *need* to understand so you can provide the most thoughtful recommendation or solution. There is nothing wrong with asking "Has something changed that has brought this to the forefront? " or "This is a problem because ..." (if it's done in a respectful manner and tone of voice!).

The first step to asking good questions is slowing down!

Truly work to understand as much as you can in the time you have to help. This will enable you to clearly demonstrate you care. The more directly related your recommendation is to solving the problem, the more clearly you'll demonstrate your value. Because — you know their stuff! And once you know their stuff, you've earned the right to talk about, examine, explore, improve, change, and build upon their stuff by applying the tricks of your trade (i.e., your stuff!).

Active Listening

You can ask all the questions in the world. They can be great questions. But if you're not listening to the answers, well, you're not learning. Active listening is also a method of demonstrating your understanding of the situation that has been presented to you. Again, I'm challenged by this competency because I tend to already be thinking of my answer instead of actively, physically listening. (Don't do this — LOL!) Or I'm forming my next question in my brain. It can be hard not to surrender to the impulse to anticipate and "be ready." But listening to respond is far less effective than listening to understand.

Stop! Slow down and honestly listen. A tip you can use, if you have an idea about what is going to be asked of you, is to prepare some questions ahead of time. You may have worked with this individual before and have an awareness of how they present challenges to you. As such, plan to be a step ahead so you have the time and confidence to listen actively to the new situation.

You can demonstrate this as simply as a statement: "I hear you saying ..." (and repeat back, in your words, what they just said). Wait for their acknowledgement or for them to correct you or add additional information. Head nods and verbal cues are other ways to demonstrate that you're actively involved in the conversation.

What if I'm "Weak" Here? — Practical Tips for Brushing Up Your "Know Your Stuff" Competencies

Building Up Your Business Acumen:

➜ Read about your industry or sector and learn as much as you can about your own operations and the inner workings of your competitors. Subscribe to and read trade magazines, industry magazines, and relevant websites. And seek opportunities to shadow colleagues in other departments so you can get smart about "their stuff" and about the culture and operations of your business from multiple angles.

Queuing Up Good Questions:

➜ Ask a mentor (and they don't have to work with you!) to push back *every time* you answer a question without asking a clarifying question first. Make sure the mentor always answers *your* questions with a question. You don't have to try this initially in high-stakes environments, but can role play this with others outside of your workplace. With some practice, you'll get really good at asking meaningful questions that advance the relationship and the work at hand. For example, if your mentor asks you, "How long will a project like this take to finish?" you might respond with, "It really depends on the breadth and depth of the deliverable you're seeking. Can you tell me more about what the executive team is hoping to see when I come give the presentation about the project? I want to ensure that my deliverable lives up to your expectations."

✦ At work, listen to yourself as you are asking questions to assess whether they are the right questions at the right times. Ask follow-up questions for clarification if you aren't 100% sure about everything that was just said to you.

✦ Draft some common questions that others ask you when seeking your assistance, then practice answering these questions with follow-ups. Answering a question with a question is not about being evasive and avoiding giving an answer; it's about gaining clarity and honoring the relationship/collaboration before rushing to an answer that's incomplete or abrupt.

Looking Out for Ways to Listen More Effectively:

✦ Coursework can be key. And sometimes it's low-cost or free! "Soft skills," like active listening, can be taught and some-times you might feel more comfortable working on these personal skills with strangers (experts!) instead of your coworkers. I just did a search on LinkedIn Learning and found almost 500 training courses about active listening. And most of these learning opportunities are interactive.

✦ In the moment of communicating, take a breath and nod. Slow down and focus on "watching" how you interact in non-challenge situations; set a goal of demonstrating active listening skills in these settings first. Listening in volatile or contentious situations is harder; give yourself the grace to work up to that expertise.

Seek to Understand: Homework Assignment #3

"Getting to Know Them, Getting to Know All About Them ..."

Exercise #1: Learning What Makes Them Tick

Ask your CEO or a member of your senior management team to tell you a little bit about what keeps them up at night. Be sure to schedule the time formally (don't do this as a drive-by or as water-cooler chatter) and set an agenda so they can be prepared to respond. Practice active listening and questioning when meeting with them. While this conversation is about them imparting insight to you, you can help them be the star of the discussion by asking smart questions, then sitting back to truly listen.

Bonus Point: Prepare a recap email, thanking them for their time, demonstrating what your heard, and letting them know how you will work to become more knowledgeable in these areas. Simply acknowledging that it was eye-opening for you to better understand what keeps leaders up at night is a great way to imply (or overtly say!) that you want to become someone who is on the lookout for ways to quell leadership discomfort in any way you can. (Do not propose solutions — yet.)

Exercise #2: Understanding the Business

Answer the following questions as it relates to the organization that employs you (or to your biggest client if you're a consultant or external provider of services):

- ➜ How does my company make money?

- ➜ What's our primary product/service? Secondary? What's on the horizon?

- ➜ Where do we lose money at the top line or profit margin at the bottom line?

- ➜ Who are our customers? What are all the different segments we *currently* serve, and else *should* we be serving?

- Where do we find our customers and how do we engage them?
- How do we lose customers or lose their enthusiastic support?
- Who are *my* internal customers who deserve my focus and intention?

Exercise #3: "Know Their Stuff" Self-Assessment

Rank yourself in each competency: Business Acumen, Questioning, and Active Listening

a. Which is your strongest? How do you demonstrate the competency daily?

____

____

____

b. Which is your weakest? How have you demonstrated this on occasion?

____

____

____

c. What actions will you take to leverage the opportunities of your strongest area and to improve your abilities in your weakest area?

____

____

____

CHAPTER 6

BUILDING BLOCK #3:
Know Your Audience

Now that you've got a solid understanding of how to "know *your* stuff" (building block #1) and "know *their* stuff" (building block #2) and why it's vital appropriately demonstrate this expertise and perspective, let's explore the third building block. You guessed it: Know your *audience*!

Knowing your audience is all about knowing how to communicate (and it's more than just good questions and active listening, which we explored in Chapter 5).

You know, you never really can (or should?) separate work and home completely. I am blessed to be married to a fabulous man; we've had more than 25 years together and are still going strong. He says it's because he just does what I say (which is true, for the most part) but it really is more than that. I think that the key to every solid relationship (at work or at home) comes down to really *understanding* one another, examining the differences that each person brings to the relationship, and then honoring those differences (and preferences) by adjusting our communications to be optimally (and respectfully) understood. We all have different "styles" and unique personalities. Believe it or not, completing an assessment to determine our DiSC® Profiles[7] was incredibly informative to our marriage and our business partnership. Barry and I had been together for some

---

7   The DiSC® Profile is a popular workplace soft-skills assessment developed by Personality Profile Solutions, LLC, and is used in many industries to help employees better understand themselves and others based on each individual's unique combination of four personality styles: dominant, influence, steadiness, and compliance. www.DiSCprofile.com

time and my company, HR Resolutions, was already in business for several years by the time we completed the work-style assessments.

The key to every solid relationship (at work or at home) comes down to really understanding one another, examining the differences that each person brings to the relationship, and then honoring those differences (and preferences) by adjusting our communications to be optimally (and respectfully) understood.

Hopefully you have already determined that I'm sociable and high energy. On the DiSC® scale, I'm considered a High-I or an "influencer." We influencers are happy people (generally), we exude energy (mostly), we talk fast (almost always), and we skim over details (ugh!). Well, Barry is non-sociable; he's not anti-social, per se, but isolation has always been his "happy place." Barry takes his time making decisions and is slow-paced (he even walks slowly — egads!). He absorbs information, then considers all the parameters, effort, and energy required, and ultimately wants to know the benefit of the action, activity, or decision.

Stop for a minute and try to picture it — married life for a high-energy, party-waiting-to-happen wife and a slow-paced, details-needed, time-taking husband. We used to get frustrated with each other all the time. I'd want to GO DO SOMETHING, or I had the GREATEST IDEA EVER. Barry would want details and I'd get frustrated because it was the BEST THING EVER … didn't he see that? (The caps here serve a purpose — I would get THAT EXCITED!) Barry would get frustrated too and he'd need me to slow the heck down because he needed processing and rumination time. It's not that he's not supportive of my AMAZING IDEAS, but simply that he's going to take longer to make a decision or support a business idea. We were both frustrated (but we didn't really realize that the reason *why* we were frustrated was this personality clash).

Insert communication-style assessment here. Finding out our DiSC®
Profiles was a watershed moment. What we each learned about ourselves
was eye opening. And the fact that we could learn to understand someone
else's style — and adjust our communication and behavior accordingly —
was a little jarring to me at first. Of course, as a human resources professional, I love people. And I love different people. But I didn't want to flex
for them. I knew my own workplace/leadership style. I communicated in
my own style — isn't that natural? Why in the world would I need to adapt
to someone *else*? Huh. For me and Barry, the minute we both truly understood the ins and outs of our personal communication styles, we were
both able to adapt and communicate *better*. Now, if I REALLY want to
do THE BEST THING EVER, I slow down; I present the facts; I give Barry
(my audience) the information in *his* natural style so he can truly hear
the message I'm trying to relay. Barry also realizes that if he gives me too
many details or doesn't get right to the point when he's trying (painstak-
ingly) to communicate something to me, my eyes are going to glaze over
and my ears will stop listening. I'll hear "blah, blah, blah" if he doesn't at
least demonstrate that he's *trying* to cut to the chase.

We interact completely differently now. Frankly, I now feel *heard,* and
Barry feels *appreciated*. We have both learned to deliver our message
in the *other person's style* so they can truly hear the message and feel
acknowledged through the communication.

Reflection Question

    Who do you work or collaborate with who has a communication style and
overall personality that's very different from your own? How has this inability to
understand your audience (i.e., for you to understand them and/or for them to
understand you) caused frustration, poor project outcomes, and even conflict?
How might you resolve current interpersonal challenges or better understand
previous ones by digging deeper in communication styles (perhaps with an
assessment, like DiSC®)? Even without the benefit of a report that outlines how
the other person is different from you, how much you start holding yourself
accountable for trying to communicate in *their* style (as you understand it)
instead of in your own default style?

When I first started studying communication styles, I questioned whether this approach wasn't a high form of manipulation or chicanery. You might be thinking that very thing right now. If I'm changing *me* just so I can persuade or influence someone's decision, am I truly being ethical, compassionate, and open-minded? Let's take a moment to consider this.

Chicanery, manipulation, "Machiavellian" — these are all words that may be used to describe changing *your* approach to influence others. Can modifying your style to influence someone else be perceived as deceptive? Absolutely. But I'm not talking about scheming and plotting. I'm talking about adapting and adjusting — ever so slightly — so you can be heard. Any over-use or misuse of a skill can lead to the wrong results.

What we really need to strive toward is delivering a message in someone else's language — in a way in which they will be able to hear and consider what we are saying so they can form their own opinion or decision. By default, most of us rely on "sender-based communications" — speaking and writing in a way that fits our own agendas and matches our own personal styles. But "receiver-based communications" is all about the audience — about their needs and perspectives, and their communications styles. By customizing our communications to others, we are opening their ears to more fully hear what we are trying to say. This, to me, is actually a form of respect for the audience — whether the "audience" is one employee (or peer or boss), a team of a few people, or a large audience like the attendees at a conference presentation.

> **"Receiver-based communications" is all about the audience — about their needs and perspectives, and their communications styles. By customizing our communications to others, we are opening their ears to more fully hear what we are trying to say.**

A Story for Learning:
How Fear of Communicating with Challenging People Can Make a Situation Worse

Many moons ago, I worked for a tyrant CEO. We'll call him David. He was rude in his dealings with others, often ignorant about the things he purported to understand, appeared as if he couldn't care less about his employees and colleagues, and was, all around, not a very nice guy. David refused to listen to anything negative about himself or any of his favored, "pet" employees. I had observed that David was resistant to taking even an iota of feedback about his management style. His approach to communicating with *others* made it very difficult, indeed, for any of us to communicate effectively with *him*.

Our company had a sister company in the same town, and our two companies often collaborated on providing programs and services for our collective employee populations. The HR director at our sister company — Walter — and I teamed up to deliver a joint sales training program after receiving a directive from our Germany headquarters about bolstering our sales skills company wide.

Walter was a trusted colleague; I trusted him, and he trusted me. We had mutual respect. Our teams completed the training session and, during the session, one of David's "pet" employees gossiped about David's management style with *all* the participants. This was brought directly to my attention by several employees who felt the comments were inappropriate and who reported that the conversations made them feel uncomfortable.

I have rarely shied away from an honest conversation about a critical workplace issue. But communicating with David was a challenge. I knew from my previous dealings with him that there was no conceivable way that he would have listened to me regarding his alleged questionable behavior *nor* that he would have believed that "his" people said something negative about him. He expected and demanded loyalty and submission, like most tyrant leaders tend to do. I felt like I needed to take a different route to opening the conversation with David about what his employees said publicly about him during the training program. So, I told David that Walter — the HR director at our sister company and my collaborator in delivering the sales training was the one who brought this concern to my attention. I thought that David might be more receptive to feedback from Walter — given that Walter was a director with human resources responsibilities and because he wasn't one of David's direct reports. David became incredibly angry and *still* did not believe it; he was sure no one would ever complain about him. He told me that he needed to talk with Walter directly. (Oh, boy. Walter wasn't the one who told me the information. I had simply used him as the scapegoat, thinking David would sit up and listen if he thought the concerns were coming from an HR director. Our angry CEO was about to pick up the phone and call Walter, perhaps attacking him about what he "said" — which he never actually said.) Naturally, I panicked.

I quickly called Walter and *begged* him to go along with the story. (I am still incredibly embarrassed sharing this.) Walter agreed to go along with the ruse, as he understood the situation I faced. Oh, what a tangled web I had woven! And it gets even messier than this. David (our CEO and my boss) went to *Walter's* boss at our sister company, complaining about "Walter gossiping." Ugh. Bit by bit, the ordeal got uglier as more people got involved. Walter was a trooper — taking a lot of unnecessary heat, all because of my creative approach to circumventing what I thought would have been a more difficult conversation with David. Walter explained the situation to his boss and, in the end, Walter still took a hit to his credibility with his boss but survived the ordeal.

I finally couldn't take it anymore — I felt awful. So, I owned up to David: "I lied — Walter never told me that; I heard it directly from several of our own employees, David, but I knew you wouldn't believe me." I'm not sure what I expected to happen once I set the record straight. But here's what *did* happen ... David never spoke another word to me again — ever. Walter also never spoke to me again, sadly. I had lost the respect, trust, and attention of my counterpart at our sister company and of my own boss. How in the world was I going to go on at this company?

I was "saved by the calendar" in that I was scheduled to be on vacation the next week *and* I got a job offer from another company. I was glad to submit my resignation *during* vacation and was relieved that David was traveling during the remainder of my final-notice period before my departure. We never saw each other after that fateful admission.

But just because I was able to essentially turn tail and run after that horrible moment in my career didn't mean it wasn't critical for me to learn from it and be better for the future. If I was ever going to be the kind of leader I aspired to be, I needed to confront the elephant in the room: I had chosen dishonesty because of my fear of communicating with someone who had proven to be difficult in the past. I had let *his* historic behavior determine my own. And I knew that "two wrongs don't make a right." Tyrant or no tyrant, I could have done better. And in the future, I would. I am proud to report that I have long since learned to *find* a way — no matter how hard it is —to make someone believe me and to earn their attention and open-mindedness during high-stakes conversations. Never again in my career would there be an impulse to make up stories that damage my credibility or the credibility of others.

As I think about Building Block #3 ("Know Your Audience") and all that I have learned over the years about communicating with people whose behavior and outlook styles are different from my own, I can't help but wonder whether having more skills in the "know your audience" arena might have changed my relationship with the tyrant boss and the trajectory of my career at that company. I suspect that if I had truly understood back then how to work with people who are different from me, I could have crafted my message for David in a way that would have been honest, clear, kind, and respectful — in a way that might have been disarming enough to allow him to hear what I was trying to say. In the end, his only takeaway was probably that his HR team had lied to him or manipulated him, when what he really needed to hear was that his daily management style was leaving his employees feeling so badly that they felt forced to commiserate about their toxic workplace when gathered together for events like training programs. The saddest thing about it all is that David probably never gained the self-awareness that "the gossiping incident" could have delivered to him about his management-style weaknesses.

Reflection Question

What major misstep(s) have you made in your career because you didn't know how to alter your communications approach to customize it to the audience? How might you do things different if you could go back in time? How might your future interactions with colleagues or clients be better if you regularly ask yourself, "What do I need to know, understand, and respect about this person or group's behavior style or communications preferences so I can be most effective in communicating with them?"

To this day, I'm mortified by the kinds of missteps I made during the early years of my career. Perhaps you are too. But as we live (and make mistakes), we learn. And if we're open to the learning, we can become more competent and professional, eventually arriving at a place where we truly *deserve* to be heard, trusted, and respected for our expertise. And yes, most sought-after experts have some battle wounds from their early learning. Failure is a breeding ground for growth. And as we grow, we fail less and less. Being sought-after is not about being perfect, and it certainly doesn't require that we started our careers with perfect judgment and maturity. If it did, none of us would make it into the leadership ranks, nor would any of us be truly "sought-after" in the way we might deserve.

Failure is a breeding ground for growth. And as we grow, we fail less and less. Being sought-after is not about being perfect, and it certainly doesn't require that we started our careers with perfect judgment and maturity.

Knowing Your Audience: Why This Building Block Is Important

Being sought-after means that people want to hear what you have to say. If you aren't speaking to your audience in a way they can actually absorb your points, they won't turn to you for assistance, leadership, insight, or guidance. Or they will turn to you only begrudgingly because they don't have a choice. (Think about when you *have to* talk with someone who you just *do not* want to interact with at work ... but they have information that you need. Or, worse yet, they're your boss!)

Some of the experts I interviewed for this book happen to believe that, next to Knowing Your Stuff (Building Block #1), the ability to communicate is paramount to being heard, being trusted, and being recognized for knowing your stuff! Kate Colbert offered the best quote:

> "If Einstein understood E=MC² but couldn't explain it to anyone, where would that have left him?"

Steve Gilliland talks about communication serving as the "synergy" or the glue for everything else:

> "Let's face it — it helps us build relationships by allowing us to share our experiences. And it helps us connect with others."

Being sought-after is exactly that — being the kind of expert who connects with (and communicates with) others in a way that leaves them *seeking* that connection from you, over and over again.

What's *Your* Communication Style?

There are too many workplace assessments in the world to name them all. A Google search for "communication style assessment" resulted in 239 million results. But let's just talk about one that many people rely upon and appreciate. Our focus in this section will be the DiSC® profile — the assessment I talked about when sharing with you some of the key behavioral and communications differences between me and my husband, Barry.

DiSC® takes into consideration many factors when determining where your primary, or natural, communication style lands as well as where you will default/adapt when under stress or unsure of your environment. (Good heavens, I get chattier when I'm under stress! How about you?)

It is very important to understand and appreciate that no one style is better than another. It's just *your* style. It's not bad to be dominant in communications, nor is there anything wrong with gathering data and considering all sides to a situation before saying much at all. We need to have high-energy, excited people in our lives; we need others who look to relate to everyone and "keep the peace." Imagine if we were all identical — ugh!

It is very important to understand and appreciate that no one style is better than another.

Let's start with the D in DiSC.® "D" is for dominance. Now, that doesn't mean the individual enters the room and dominates the conversation, not letting anyone else get a word in edgewise. What this refers to is how a person relays and receives information. A "D" personality will need bullet points and no extraneous fluff — you usually have to get to the point when working with people who are considered "high Ds." You can sometimes quickly uncover a "D" in emails; do they send short, to-the-point communications? Are there bullet points? Do they completely bypass a salutation or just use your first name? That is a "D" for sure! If you want a "D" to seek you out, then respond in kind — straight to the point. Adapt to their preference, skipping over the small-talk and getting right to business. With a high D, it's usually best not to discuss the weekend and your upcoming plans. They want the answers to their questions — not an unsolicited story or your thoughts about the weather. It's not that they don't care about you — about your son's Bar Mitzvah or your spouse's new job; it's just that your personal life or your broken-down car probably aren't relevant in that moment. The meeting theme or agenda is what drives the discussion for a high D. Speak in their language — even by cutting to the chase and skipping the salutation in your emails. If you mirror their style, you may find you are getting faster responses *and* they will seek you out again! High Ds appreciate people who, like them, appear to be "all about the work."

Next in the DiSC® framework is the "I" for influence. A person who is a "high I" may very well enter the room and dominate the conversation, ready to "influence" and be influenced; heck, they want *everyone* involved in the conversation. A close colleague of mine refers to high Is (like me) as "the party waiting to happen!" An "I" will talk fast, be animated, and will include the "fluff" in communications. We want to get to the point, like a "D," but we're OK having fun getting there. Our communications, even in emails, will often include a friendly salutation, full and detailed sentences, and evidence of high energy *and* interest in life, work, the relationship and even the weather — high I personalities often deliver more than just "the message." Do your best to respond to an "I" in the same manner; this can be really challenging for other styles, as the "I" is, in my opinion, the chattiest of all the styles. An "I" will often physically seek you out in your cubicle/office or at the water cooler, if you work in the same physical location. Influencers loved the face-to-face dynamic of an office or other non-virtual workplace (and they may have struggled the most with the isolation of the pandemic — I suspect someone is doing an interesting research study on this very phenomenon).

Now we have the "S" or Steadiness in DiSC®. People with this primary style want everyone to get along and they will do all they can to ensure that happens. High S personalities are sometimes called "steady relators" and are official and unofficial conciliators and mediators, always looking for the middle ground — the happy medium and the negotiated consensus. All stakeholders need to be involved in an "S" decision. People with "S" styles are geared toward people relations but tend to be introverts — they really like to keep the peace. Conflict is unnerving for them. When communicating with a high S, I recommend that you present information in a slower and steadier pace, and ask an "S" a lot of questions for their input. They may not automatically offer their own opinions or insights, but they have a lot to say about what will work and how things affect people. John Dame, one of the sought-after experts I interviewed for this book, shared an interesting bit of information about this style; he told me that people with a high S on the DiSC® profile are "40% of the population but are the least understood."

Last, but not least, is the "C" for conscientiousness. Conscientious thinkers will give you every known fact available at the time of the communication; they want you to have every piece of information you *may* need when interacting. Their emails, reports, presentations, and voice messages tend to be long and involved. They need to receive the same level of response to hear the incoming message. When communicating with a high C personality, do your best to supply as much information and as many facts as possible. If you don't have all the relevant details in your original communication, it's helpful to assure your high-C counterpart that you are available to answer questions or provide additional information, if needed (or that you'll be following up with them soon with additional information). Think of a high-C interaction this way: give them all the "data" and backstory they might possibly need to feel comfortable in the relationship or situation. If it's relevant, it's worth mentioning.

"Knowing your audience" and knowing how to communicate effectively with them is a vital component of becoming sought-after for your expertise. Recognizing that different people have different preferences for communications is important. Familiarizing yourself with different personality styles can be a good place to "level up" your skills in this regard. The DiSC® profile is just one of many workplace assessments that can help us better understand one another. And before we move on, I think it's important enough to say it again: no one style is better than another. We have a natural style, which is easy and automatic for us, and a secondary style that also comes quite naturally. You may find that, like me, you have very little of one or two of the styles in your toolbox. Some people are all D and I, with almost no S and C, or very high S and C with almost no D or I. There is nothing wrong with that. Further, it is also rare that your style will change a whole lot during your career. It may morph depending upon your position. For example, when I'm serving as the "HR director" in my own business, I'm a significantly higher "I." But, when I'm acting and making decisions as "president" of my company, I tend to become more "D," especially as I've grown in the role. (For what it's worth, "D" is also my fallback — it's my style when I'm tired or lazy or distracted.)

Think about situations in which your audience has responded in a positive way to information you presented. Perhaps it was a difficult situation with an employee that ended well. Or maybe it was a presentation to a client, where they seemed highly engaged and grateful. In these moments, you will find clues to their communication style. As you seek to better understand the various audiences you interact with, don't forget to analyze your own style too. Dig deep and discover what about *you* was different in scenarios where things went well versus moments when things fell apart. Taking a close look at the high points and low points in your interpersonal interactions will start to give you clues about *their* communication style and *yours* as well. And when you know your audience *and* you know yourself, your results will show it.

"Know Your Audience" Competencies

In some ways, career success is all about interpersonal communications and interactions. That's why it doesn't surprise me that, in my experience, the "know your audience" competencies — the know-how necessary for effective communications — can take a little longer to master and to gain comfort with.

Sought-after experts who "know their audience" tend to have strong competencies when it comes to:

- ➤ Observation
- ➤ Listening for Clues
- ➤ Adapting
- ➤ Honesty.

Let's dig into these competencies to see how to level-up your communications skills.

Observation

It surely takes some practice to become comfortable reading someone else's communication style. The best method is to just observe how the person talks to you and others. Compare various written messages and communications. What do you notice? Are they a "just the facts" communicator or do their words seem to demonstrate a focus on the relationship and the contexts, not just the transactional purpose of the email, phone call, or conversation? As you become adept at recognizing the communication styles of others, start to look at situations when it seems they may change (e.g., when I let my staff know I'm in "D" mode and to please not be offended if I'm abrupt or less than friendly). As you observe the communications behaviors and preferences of others, don't forget to pay attention to body language.

Individuals also prefer how they receive communications or "VAK"[8]: visual, auditory, or kinesthetic (touch/feel) input. This is the sensory way someone learns/understands or hears better. There is absolutely nothing wrong with asking someone how they best learn: "hearing" the message, "seeing" the message," or actually "doing" the task to be learned. Pay attention to whether someone is an "auditory learner," if they prefer to read/study the information that comes to them, or if they learn best by hands-on practice. Auditory learning, visual learning, and experiential learning can be appreciated all by the same person, but people typically have a preferred method for receiving information and processing it.

Listening for Clues

In this book, we've talked a lot about the power of effective listening. And here we go again. When it comes to mastering the "know your audience" building block, you should be listening for clues to someone's communication/behavior style (such as their DiSC® profile) and sensory style (VAK). Trigger words can help you identify their learning/hearing style. For example:

➔ Karen, I *hear* you are going to be presenting to the Board next week. Susan was telling me all about it. (Auditory learning)

➔ Karen, I *see* you are going to be presenting to the Board next week. There's a poster about it in then cafeteria and Susan sent out an email announcement. (Visual learning)

➔ Karen, let's click through your Board presentation in advance. (Kinesthetic learning)

---

8 https://thepeakperformancecenter.com/educational-learning/learning/preferences/learning-styles/vak/

Stop and take a minute to review your own learning style — if you're not sure, look at the words you use when you communicate: are you "hearing," "seeing," or "experiencing/trying" things?

Adapting

Once you uncover someone's communication style, you should adapt your messaging and delivery style accordingly. This can be challenging because what works for one person might not work for the rest of the team or the whole audience. There is no way you can speak to everyone in a conference audience or in a room with more than a dozen people. In this situation, your job is to include as many of the methodologies as possible: spoken (verbal with varying delivery tones), visual presentation (visual with varying styles), and interactive (kinesthetic experiences — like passing something around the room or the crowd, or inviting people to come close for some sort of demonstration — for those who need to "touch" the message.) Group emails are another challenge, but approaching group emails are a challenge that can be overcome; I recommend you use a toned down "natural" (to you) style when sending one email message to multiple recipients who have different styles.

Adapting your communication style for the people in front of you is a way to truly honor and respect your audience. If they cannot fully hear and appreciate (and perhaps even respond to and act upon) your message, both you and your audience will become frustrated ... and frustration in the absence of true communication and understand creates a spiral of disappointment.

Honesty

In this book, we've talked a lot about honesty, authenticity, and vulnerability. And when it comes to Sought-After Building Block #3 — Know Your Audience — it's imperative that your approach to that audience and your communications with each audience be based on honesty. We've been talking here about adapting your approach or style of communication to align with the preferences of the audience and let me reiterate that adapting your *style* to your audience is not a means of deception. More importantly, if you want to become sought-after for your counsel and expertise, you must ensure that your actual messages are truthful. The more difficult the truth of the matter is for someone to hear, the more important it is for your communication style to match. Someone who is a "straight to the point" communicator will appreciate you ripping the proverbial bandage off when sharing difficult news, but someone who is very relationship focused is likely to prefer that same news to be delivered in the contexts of some reassurances about what the difficult news does and doesn't mean for the long-term relationship. Part of becoming sought-after is establishing your credibility. Do so in an honest and forthright manner, in a way that lets your message be fully heard.

Think about times when you've been fed a line of bull — when someone beat around the bush or buttered you up disingenuously or outright lied to you. How did that make you feel? You most likely could see right through the delivery and it's unlikely you trusted that individual after that moment. As I learned with the "David and Walter debacle," lying or being in any way deceptive can be "career-ending."

The beauty of committing to being an honest communicator is that it's the path of least resistance. It's easy. When you believe in your message, there is really no need to stretch the truth. No one is served well and, frankly, the long-term damage to a reputation can be worse than the short-term gain of bending the truth or avoiding an important issue to save face or protect someone's feelings.

What if I'm "Weak" Here? — Practical Tips for Brushing Up Your "Know Your Audience" Competencies

If you think you might be weak when it comes to knowing your audience and communicating in synch with their style, you should take comfort in knowing you are not alone! Here's how to master Building Block #3:

1. **Assess and learn your own style first.** Become comfortable talking about your preferences, habits, strengths, and weaknesses. Taking an assessment, like the DiSC® Profile, can be a great avenue toward these insights.

2. **Assess and learn the style of someone else.** Choose a close confidante, teammate, family member, or mentor, and ask them about their style. They might even know their DiSC® style and be excited to talk to you about it.

3. **Practice adapting your style** to the "practice" person or group that you've been assessing.

    a. Make notes about what worked and what didn't.

    b. Ask for constructive feedback and for the ability to talk about it, in a safe environment where humility and humor are welcome.

4. **Expand your practice to those you want to reach daily.** If you want to be sought-after by your boss's boss, or among top clients, or with the employees in a department in your company that you think could benefit from your collaborations, start going out of your way to communicate with them more deliberately. Remember to flex your style to suit *their* needs.

5. **Give yourself some grace, knowing that you're a work in progress.** Understanding your audience and nailing your communications strategy for each audience in your orbit is difficult work. In fact, this is probably the toughest building block to master. And it might take your entire career. Keep at it!

➤ Seek to Understand: Homework Assignment #4

Honing Your Communications Skills to Meet Your Audience Where They Are

Exercise #1: Know Thyself

Determine, informally or formally, your natural communication style. Identify colleagues with different styles and prepare your own examples of how each naturally communicates *and* how you will communicate with them moving forward.

_____

_____

_____

_____

Bonus Point: Discuss communications styles and preferences, in detail, with one of the colleagues you just identified and seek their input and feedback on how you can flex your style to the people around you. Ask them: "Help me understand how you like to communicate."

Exercise #2: Study Your Customer Avatar

Bring to mind one specific person who you really want to seek you out. It can be a colleague who you want to serve and impress; it could be a prospective client; it might be an association or public figure who you'd like to share a stage with. Compile a set of communications in their voice (emails, memos, videos, website copy, social media posts, etc.) — anything you can find that they wrote or said. Think of them as your "customer avatar" — the person or figure who represents your goal when it comes to the kinds of audiences you want to serve. Study your customer avatar's style and word choices; make notes about how they present themselves (verbally, in writing, and in terms of body language or presence). Assign one of the four DiSC® styles to them, based on your current knowledge about the four styles and knowing that it's just a guess (unless you work for a company that publishes the DiSC® profiles of all its people (some companies do this, which is really helpful!). Complete more detailed research on their style and how to best interact with them, if possible.

Draft responses and/or comments to the compiled communications. You're not necessarily ever going to share these responses with them — this is just an exercise. Then review the sample communications and responses with your mentor or a trusted colleague. If possible, do this review with someone who actually knows your customer avatar and who even has the "ear" of that individual.

Bonus Point: Ask the person you have identified as your customer avatar, if possible and if you're comfortable doing so, for a time to chat about how you can be of service to them. Consider providing them, in *their* style, a summary of what you have learned about your differing styles *and* how you'll communicate moving forward. This conversation doesn't have to be creepy. No need to be all "So I've been reading every memo you've ever written and studying you late at night." Try saying, "One of my personal development goals is to better flex and adapt my communication style to other people. You're someone I'd like to ensure I'm doing that for. It seems to me, when I read your emails and hear you speaking at meetings, that you're very relationship focused and care a lot about background information, contexts, and possibilities. I tend to be a minimalist when it comes to communicating — sharing just a quick update or cutting right to the chase without emphasizing the relationship or a fuller context. How do you think I can do a better job of communicating with you in a way that matches your own preferences?"

Exercise #3: "Know Your Audience" Self-Assessment

Rank yourself in each competency: Observation, Listening for Clues, Adapting, and Honesty.

    a.   Which is your strongest? How do you demonstrate the competency daily?

        _____

        _____

        _____

        _____

b. Which is your weakest? How have you demonstrated this
    on occasion?

    _____

    _____

    _____

    _____

c. What actions will you take to leverage the opportunities of
    your strongest area and to improve your abilities in your
    weakest area?

    _____

    _____

    _____

    _____

CHAPTER 7

BUILDING BLOCK #4: Be Flexible

J ust like death and taxes, change is inevitable. But *unlike* death and taxes, change doesn't have to be something you constantly seek to avoid or evade. People who are truly "sought-after" for their expertise are often those who embrace and even champion change. And champions for change are, in a word, flexible. The pandemic taught many businesses and individuals the importance of the ability to "pivot" (sometimes by a few degrees and sometimes by 180 degrees) to get through the changes that were out of our control. The type of change required during crisis can be massive, but now that things might be getting "back to normal" at your company and in your career, it would be foolish to assume that your change-making days are behind you. For people, products, and organizations to remain relevant and viable, change is necessary nearly every day. And change is an opportunity to set yourself apart. Managers manage change; leaders strategize change; those who are sought-after *embrace change*. For flexible experts who champion change, change doesn't deplete us — it gives us energy and it challenges us to find a way through and to make the best of any situation.

> Managers manage change; leaders strategize change; those who are sought-after *embrace change*.

Reflection Question

Do you love or hate — embrace or resist — change? Take a moment and think about how you handle change. Where can a mindset shift help you champion change (for the first time or even more than you already do)? Did you know that people who are risk averse and resistant to change can, over time, become energized and motivated by change? How you feel about change can change!

While change is inevitable, it's also important to not initiate change for change's sake — you know, "if it ain't broke, don't fix it." Make change when, and only when, change promises to drive progress or growth. Great leaders are always looking for changes that might result in better employee relations, larger market share and exposure, quality improvement for a better product, economies and efficiencies for a better business model. If something is good for the people you serve (customers, employees, etc.), good for the world, and good for your bottom line, it might be a change worth pursuing.

Work hard to not say "Here we go again" when your manager or leader comes up with a great idea. If you want to be sought-after, be open-minded and curious. That might require that you, at first, be quiet. Have the argument internally with all the reasons "it won't work." Breathe. Then, if you still believe "here we go again," it is also your job to challenge your manager or leader. *But do so privately.* Have your business case ready to go (in their preferred communication manner — "know your audience!"). Have the discussion about all the reasons "it won't work." But be 100% sure they fully understand that, at the end of the day, you will support their decision and help them drive the change forward. The more they understand you will not be an impediment, the more they will listen to your arguments. You may very well have valid concerns and even evidence that the proposed change might not work, and the only way for you to champion the change is if you get your concerns addressed. So, make sure you have completely addressed the internal arguments you have had with yourself — get them all out of your system, respectfully, appropriately, and privately. Don't let your fears or concerns about the change turn you into a gossiper or a saboteur. Say your piece[9] — you *should* learn to surface questions and concerns at the outset of a big initiative if you want to become sought-after. (Yep, it's scary at first. And asking "But what about?" at the beginning is far better than being the person who says nothing until the "I could have told you so" in the end, if things don't go well.) Championing change often requires that we first question and fully understand it.

The next thing to do is support your leadership team's[10] decision publicly and help them drive change forward. Once the change initiative is underway, it's no one else's business that you once disagreed with the decision (and might still have misgivings). It's your job to agree with the decision, the process, and the desired change. Be the leadership team's ally no matter what your peers and your colleagues have to say.

If the change doesn't work, don't you dare say, "I told you so." Never, ever, under any circumstances (except in your own mind). Being "that guy" — the "sour grapes" person who draws attention to themselves as being smarter than the leaders whose change initiative failed — is not a good look. Again, support the change by doing a deep dive into *why* it didn't work, what elements of the change were beneficial and are worth further investigation or investment, and what to do *now*. Don't be passive aggressive either, using phrases like "as we discussed in our one-on-one ..." or "you're aware that I had these concerns." That's not any different from saying "I told you so."

Let me share a funny and relevant story. I have a long-time client who sometimes pushes boundaries and works in the gray areas of HR — tiptoeing around legal regulations, safety standards, and best practices

---

9   I always thought it was "Say your peace" but it's actually "Say your piece." This phrase is commonly confused with "Speak now or forever *hold your peace*." But keeping quiet (i.e., holding your peace) isn't the same thing as "saying your piece" (i.e., sharing a piece of information or expressing an opinion). Please tell me I'm not the only one who just learned this! Ah, there are lessons aplenty when writing (and editing) a book.

10   This advice is equally applicable for aspiring and sought-after external consultants. Once a client or prospective client understands your concerns and has answered your questions, it's your job to support the change if they decide to move forward and if you're still a part of the team or project. If a client wants to initiate a change that you disagree with so vehemently that you believe their actions are out of alignment with your values, then remove yourself from the project or the overall relationship. But when it comes to change, if you're in it, you need to support it.

for hiring, firing, and managing people. My job as their HR advisor is to provide options for them and outline the associated risks of each option; it's the client's job to make the decision. My team and I at HR Resolutions then fully support and implement their decision (as long as it's in the clear or in the gray areas — we would never support or take part in anything that's illegal or unethical). During one of the fated moments when my client wanted to traipse into a gray area, I offered options with associated risks, and he chose my least preferred option — one that had some significant risk attached to it. Lo and behold, his decision backfired (and it cost him more than $100,000). To this day, I still remember him telling me the outcome. His next sentence was, "Go ahead … say it." Seriously clueless as to what he expected me to say, I asked him what he meant. He offered a few more "Go ahead … I know, I know. You can say it," then finally said "Come on. I know you want to say, 'I told you so!'" Unwaveringly, I told him he will never hear that out of my mouth. I never said it. Now, do you think I was *thinking* it? Oh, you betcha!

A Story for Learning: Being a "Good Corporate Citizen" Even When You Quietly Disagree

These days, I like to think of myself as a champion for change — someone who is willing to let go of old practices and processes to seize something better. I like to think I'm flexible and that my stances are pliable, while my values are stable. But not all change is good change (or properly timed change), and there have been plenty of times in my career when I have been a voice of dissent.

Many moons ago, during my tenure with a manufacturing organization owned by a big German company, we launched/ implemented two different performance-review programs in the mere two years I was there. Keep in mind that translates to three different systems for reviewing employee performance: the system that was in place when I started, the one rolled out shortly after I started, and the "new and improved" one. Granted, the new and improved one (we'll call that #3 for simplicity's sake) was really good. The project started with establishing the goals of the US president; these goals were determined in collaboration with our international parent company. Goals were developed by considering International's expectations and the US president's strategic plans for the upcoming year. These goals were published throughout the company. Next, the US president's senior managers were expected to set their own personal performance goals based upon the leader's goals. These management-level performance goals were published. We kept going down the corporate food chain — level by level — to the entry-level floor technicians and machinists. Everyone's performance would be based upon their successful achievement of their pre-established goals which, in theory, would drive the company's (and international parent company's) goals forward. Right?

Absolutely brilliant ... in theory. But we had big problems:

➜ **Problem #1:** People, including the US president, didn't want "International" involved in our local goals and performance management.

➜ **Problem #2:** People, including the US president, were tired of the "next, newest, and greatest thing" to come from the International Office. We were systemically exhausted by the idea of another new system for reviewing, measuring, and documenting employee performance.

➜ **Problem #3:** Do you know how long it takes to do something like this successfully? Did I mention that the people were exhausted?

➜ **Problem #4:** The US president of our company, publicly with his leadership, made a statement that sounded a little like this: "Someone must have read a new management book and thought , 'Ah ha! Brilliant! Now we have to change our review system — *again!*'"

Frankly, as the HR manager responsible for helping drive this significant project, I was a little leery as well. Leery or not, my responsibility was to support and drive the new performance-review system forward regardless of the roadblocks put in my way from all sources. It *really* didn't help that the president was publicly against it. I needed his support. In all honestly, in private meetings with the president, I agreed completely with all his points and concerns. However, publicly, in front of leadership and employees, I needed to support and, in fact, *tout* the change as a great move forward for the organization. Ideally, the president would have acted in the same fashion but, alas, I was not heard, trusted, or recognized by him yet — LOL! (Oh, our early careers were so painful, weren't they?)

To make a long story short, let me just say that the process failed miserably. The president was able to use the drama of the failure to his advantage with the international parent company "powers that be" to say: "See? Your idea didn't work in the US; we do things differently here." But our failure wasn't about US culture and it wasn't about the performance-review system itself (which was actually quite good).

So, why did the process fail? It was because we lacked the appropriate champions for change — we didn't have people at the top who were flexible and open-minded. To be fair, the lack of support from the US leadership team wasn't the entire cause of our failure, but it was a big part. If the leaders had fully embraced the change, they could have made it work even with the inherent flaws. They *chose* to fail by choosing not to embrace the change; it was the perfect example of a self-fulfilling prophecy!

Why Is Change So Difficult?

For all the ways in which I will encourage you to be flexible in your work and to be open to change — challenging yourself to champion it — I'll be the first to admit that change is hard. And experts in this arena have done an excellent job helping us understand why.

According to Ken Blanchard, author and leadership expert, there are many reasons why change is hard. Blanchard's list of reasons translates roughly into these sentiments:[11]

1. Doing something different is awkward. At work and at home, we are creatures of habit and our minds and our bodies will resist change.

2. When faced with change, people think first about what they will lose. The status quo is comfortable.

3. Employees may feel disconnected, wondering "Why me?" even if an entire team or organization is coping with the same change.

4. It takes energy to manage change. The more change, the more tired your people will become.

5. People are at different "places" in their ability to accept and tolerate change. Change champions can be critical of those who are resisting change, and the resistors can feel overwhelmed and even oppressed by the words and behaviors of the champions.

6. Employees may believe that change requires them to do more — that the change is just one more thing to add to their over-loaded "to-do" list. Managing a big change feels like wearing yet another proverbial hat.

7. When the focus on the change ends, it's much easier to revert to old actions and behaviors. So it's hard for change to succeed because we're hardwired to revert to the status quo.

"Understand that change is slow," John Dame told me when I interviewed him for this book. "It will make people uncomfortable." He acknowledges that "no one likes change" but we can get more comfortable with the change when we understand *why* a change is being pursued. "Understand why it has to occur," John recommends. As I suggested before, it's your job to challenge and question leadership so you can contribute to important decisions and help support them. When you work to understand the

---

11 https://www.linkedin.com/pulse/7-common-reactions-change-how-respond-them-ken-blanchard/

why behind big changes, you can look to the future with the mindset of a champion or promoter rather than a detractor.

Being Flexible: Why This Building Block Is Important

Remember when we spoke about what the CEO loses sleep over? Change is one of those things. Your CEO or leader knows that no one likes change, and you can rest assured that your leaders don't want to implement change just because they have the power to do so. Your leader will be just as subject to the seven ideas shared above also; leaders are humans and, like you, they're hardwired for the status quo too. Ed Staub, one of the sought-after experts I interviewed during the writing of this book, believes that 80% of becoming sought-after is the ability to embrace change. He told me, "Change is a paradigm shift; you cannot change your *behavior* until you change the way you *think.*" This fully supports the need to understand the change and to look for the positives for focus. Change *your* mindset to help others adapt to the change that's coming.

Change *your* mindset to help others adapt to the change that's coming.

Leaders also know that they will inevitably have their "yes-people" and their "naysayers." Be their supporter and their advocate while still being true to yourself and the organization. Have the honest and real conversation, privately, about your concerns. Publicly? This is the *best* idea your leader has ever had. Demonstrate that you are in their corner. No matter what. (OK – not always. If they are proposing to break the law or do something immoral, that's a completely different beast. That's not what I'm talking about.) You will gain your leader's respect by (1) the challenge and (2) the support. Show your interest and your passion, then show your competence and commitment.

Getting there — to that place where *accepting* and even *championing* change is second nature to you — isn't easy and it takes time. When

Steve Gilliland, who wrote this book's foreword, was asked, "What advice would you give to 'up and comers' about change?" he provided something very powerful:

> "You need to understand that change is, absolutely, unequivocally their future. Change is inevitable and growth is optional."

Keep a list of the "7" readily available. Feel your own "feels" — the resistance, fear, frustration, exhaustion, indignance, and more — through each of those areas before you turn to support your leader and the people impacted by the change. Be ready to provide the support each stakeholder needs; start by becoming sought-after for your support, encouragement, and honest feedback. Continue demonstrating that you are embracing the change!

Be ready to provide the support each stakeholder needs; start by becoming sought-after for your support, encouragement, and honest feedback.

You may not be comfortable approaching the change initiator — the person or leader who is at the helm of the change that's underway or on the horizon — for an honest private conversation (at least not at first). Try it anyway. Your best bet here is to be prepared. Have your talking points ready to go; be careful to remove the emotion from your conversation. Talk honestly about each point of concern; present the business case for "why" this is a concern. Be prepared for pushback; you may need several business arguments. But also, be prepared to compromise and suggest alternatives. The best-laid plans are often developed through collaborations like these.

Ed Staub, one of the experts interviewed for this book, had the "best quote ever" for getting there when it comes to becoming a change maker. When asked what advice *he* would give an "up and comer" about being presented with a directive or news about a big change, he suggested that embracing change is a skill we can learn to demonstrate immediately. "How soon after an employee is told about a change should they be endeavoring to embrace it?" I asked Ed. And Ed simply replied, "Start by the time you end that conversation." Golden!

"Be Flexible" Competencies

Embracing change isn't easy. It requires deliberate attitudes, commitments, and skills. And it takes practice. The critical competencies for becoming a champion for change are:

- ➔ Transparency
- ➔ Discretion
- ➔ Positivity
- ➔ Energy.

Let's explore, in detail, how you can become rock-solid in the competencies required in Building Block #4.

Transparency

You absolutely need to be completely transparent when presenting your concerns and disagreement to the initiating change agent (the person who brought the plan forward). Now is not the time to downplay your concerns as a person and as an employee, particularly if you are responsible for driving the change. Get your concerns off your chest so you can move forward as well. There is no way you will sincerely be able to embrace and promote the change if you have not had your say.

But do so privately.

Discretion

To be sought-after, you cannot go along with the pack. You must know who you can speak to honestly and openly. You need to maintain confidences as well as your own personal opinions if those opinions don't advance the initiative or support the wellbeing of the team or the organization. I can disagree with something personally but still professionally support the action. Even your best confidante in the organization should not know how you really feel if you cannot fully get on board with the proposed change. Keep your negative conversations to no more than one or two people. Everyone else should see you moving the change forward — 100%. All this is not to say that you should pretend to love something that rubs you the wrong way. Having discretion isn't about being dishonest; you can do the work and say to your colleagues, "Here's what I think the best way forward looks like and here's what my team can do to help ..." without saying — one way or the other — whether you're "excited" about this change or "dreading" it. Having discretion is an important part of being flexible in the face of change. It's about having the maturity to throw yourself into the work without throwing yourself into a disagreement, a gossip-fest, or a bout of fear-mongering.

Think about the boss who told anyone who would listen how he completely disagreed with the new performance-review program. Had he kept his thoughts to only those closest to him, the project may not have been set up to fail as badly as it did.

Positivity

It's possible to exercise discretion and still be negative. Think about someone who rolls their eyes and says "No comment" when you ask what they think of the big change at work. So, it's key — if you want to be the kind of sought-after expert who others gravitate toward — that you learn to be positive in the face of change. Being a change maker isn't always as good as being a change *champion*. So, whether you agree with or disagree with the change (or the intent behind it), if you are a key player in the initiative, you must be positive and upbeat about the change when you are in front of others. You know and I know, the naysayers will pick up on any iota of doubt or negative energy from your participation. Find the positives and promote those; answer the negatives with the positive, no matter how small the positive may be. I could get into a lot of sappy phrases about positivity — you know, silver linings and all that, but I know you know what I'm talking about here. Chin up. Attitude is contagious.

Energy

Along with positivity, you must have energy to embrace change. Sometimes you must dig deep to find energy and enthusiasm, but they matter during a major change initiative. Remember that you are the cheerleader here … Have you ever seen a low-energy, negative cheerleader? How would the team move forward without the right assurances and the well-timed pep talks and pats on the back? Show others how you are embracing the change and why. Keep in mind that the more you privately disagree with the concept of the change, the more energy your public persona will need. Be ready and move the plan forward!

It takes a lot of energy to be energetic. Be well rested, watch your "comfort food" intake (and calories), and be careful with the caffeine too. While a caffeine boost can help at times, the downslide from that boost can make you fall "harder" and drain your energy faster. I speak from experience here!

Also keep in mind that "introverts need downtime to reorganize," according to John Dame, one of the experts interviewed for this book. Think of the energy it takes for an introvert to be in front of people; compound that with the energy needed to drive change. Whew — I'm tried just writing that!

Another thing that can help maintain your energy level is hydration. How do you think distance runners keep going all those miles? They must stay hydrated (and maintain food intake as well) to keep going. Consider yourself the intellectual equivalent of an elite runner when you are enacting change. Frankly, it may even help to study key tips from elite runners. Every change effort is a marathon, not a sprint. Be prepared to go the distance.

Every change effort is a marathon, not a sprint. Be prepared to go the distance.

What if I'm "Weak" Here? — Practical Tips for Brushing Up Your "Be Flexible" Competencies

Too much change can and will make anyone weak in this area. Being flexible and open to change is hard, and there is only so much positivity and energy to go around. And, as it turns out, discretion and transparency can be taxing too. I encourage you to do the exercises below to improve your ability to embrace change. And keep the following "change champion" life hacks in mind as well:

1. **Practice makes perfect.** If you are weak in "courageous conversations," practice with someone you trust but disagree with. Let them know you are practicing a new approach and want their feedback.

2. **Study change theory.** (Ugh — theory!) I love this comment from Molly West and Liz Fosselien in the *Harvard Business Review* article "Managers, What Are You Doing About Change Exhaustion?" [12] "Adopt the mantra, 'I am a person who is learning.'" Use the mantra! Say it out loud that you are learning. And when you embrace the idea of being a *student* of change, it won't be long before you're a *champion* for change!

---

12 https://hbr.org/2022/05/managers-what-are-you-doing-about-change-exhaustion

Seek to Understand: Homework Assignment #5

Flexing Your Flexibility Muscles to Become a Champion for Change

Exercise #1: Take Time Out to Reflect

What was the last difficult *and* last successful change in which you were involved? Do a deep dive into both and determine what worked and what didn't work. In particular, focus on what you remember about your personal feelings, beliefs, and emotions. Did any of these factors differ between the difficult and the successful scenario? Do you bring a different self to changes you welcome versus changes that scare you?

_____

_____

_____

_____

Bonus Point: Do a "debrief" with the "change initiator" and discuss what worked well and what could have been done differently. Give yourselves the opportunity to flex your "change muscles" together.

Exercise #2: Begging to Differ

Using a particularly difficult change scenario, draft your business case argument for "why" the change should not be implemented. Have several reasons or supporting points for each area of concern. Roleplay with a trusted colleague so you can be better prepared to have conversations of this nature in the future.

Bonus Point: Roleplay with the "change initiator" and request constructive criticism.

Exercise #3: "Be Flexible" Self-Assessment

Rank yourself in each competency: Transparency, Discretion, Positivity, and Energy.

a. Which is your strongest? How do you demonstrate the competency daily?

    _____

    _____

    _____

    _____

b. Which is your weakest? How have you demonstrated this on occasion?

    _____

    _____

    _____

    _____

c. What actions will you take to leverage the opportunities of your strongest area and to improve your abilities in your weakest area?

    _____

    _____

    _____

    _____

CHAPTER 8

Pulling It All Together

Why do you think doctors and attorneys make hundreds or even thousands of dollars an hour? Because they have worked to become trusted advisors. And they have demonstrated to their key audiences that their perspectives, skills, talents, and opinions are incredibly valuable.

What else do doctors and attorneys have in common? They all went to college for a long time, studied hard for licensure exams, were mentored and put through the paces during their first years in practice, and were given safe "practice fields" to hone their crafts over a long period of time. Before an individual can become even a little bit "sought-after" as an attorney or physician, they must meet rigorous and even grueling educational and training requirements. In thinking about this path from aspiring doctor to board-certified provider or future lawyer to state-licensed attorney, what can we *all* apply to our sought-after journey?

Doctors must spend time as interns and residents before they are set loose to see patients on their own. They work with others who are sought-after every day until they are authorized and ready to call the shots with patients on their own. Why isn't it second nature for us to do the same in our careers in other professions? I was blessed with people who recognized my talent before I even did — they mentored me and helped me become the HR professional I am today. As a consultant, author, and speaker, I regularly surround myself with others who are sought-after

— not because I want to be just like them but because I want to *learn* from them. I value and welcome their input. I look to their guidance because they paved the way before I started along the way. (And, no, they aren't even all older than me — they just started earlier in their careers than I did or ascended the career ladder quickly and have a lot to teach.)

Sought-After at Work

If you've been working for at least a few years, you've probably had the experience of offering a suggestion at work and being shot down ... then, a few months or years later, a highly paid consultant makes the exact same suggestion, your boss thinks it's brilliant. Sheesh — these outsiders make more money than you *and* they get more respect. We've all been there. But the good news is that you don't have to go start your own company or work as a consultant to get the attention and acclaim you deserve. You can be heard at work; you can be trusted at work; you can be respected for your expertise at work. You do not need to be an outsider or "consultant" for any of these conditions to occur.

You *do* need to know *your* stuff, know *their* stuff, know how to communicate with different kinds of audiences, and know how to embrace change (even when you don't agree with it).

The biggest professional lesson I have learned to date came from that career-defining moment with the VP when I said "no" about his request to fire a salesperson essentially "on the spot." I had not yet learned the importance of positioning myself so that I could be heard, be trusted, and be respected for my expertise. I was too busy following the "rules" and not considering the business needs or my audience.

Another hard lesson I had to learn was that, even as an "internal" HR professional, I was still a *consultant* within the business, and I needed to be in that mindset to truly serve my colleagues. At the end of the day, I was not a business decision maker (until I became president of my own company). I was an internal consultant — I needed to provide guidance, options, risks, observations, support, and ideas. I needed to enable others to make informed (and better) decisions. I needed to demonstrate that "my stuff" could impact "their stuff." I needed to deliver that information in a way they could truly hear and process. Once they "got it," my job was done at that point (unless and until I was needed to implement the decision being made). It took me *a long time* to not take it personally if my expert opinion wasn't followed. Kate Colbert, the marketing expert I interviewed for this book, offers a tip in this regard. She says:

> "I used to feel disrespected or unseen when my 'first drafts' were thrown away or my ideas weren't fully validated by decision-makers. And then I realized that those drafts and initial ideas provided my colleagues *a context in which to think.* And that context sometimes helped them see 'No, that's exactly the opposite of what we ought to do' or 'Yes, this is close ... *and* what we should *also* do or say is ...' The leaders and peers who would use my ideas as a jumping-off point — I now understand — often would have been entirely unable to arrive at their decision if not for my initial stab at it. What ends up on the proverbial cutting-room floor does influence the end product. These days, I consider it a privilege to offer up words and strategies to those who don't know how to get started when they're staring at a blank page. I'm not always going to nail it for the people I consult to, but I can take away the overwhelming fear of the blank page for them. 'Let me give you something to react to' is one of my favorite things to offer up to my stakeholders who find the act of getting started truly intimidating."

I needed to enable others to make informed (and better) decisions. I needed to demonstrate that "my stuff" could impact "their stuff."

Being an internal consultant — and truly seeing yourself that way — can be an important step in becoming sought-after. But what does it mean to be a consultant? Consultants, if you ask most corporate employees, are generally thought to be "outside people" who make the big bucks to come in, take everybody's time, present a solution that just won't work and/ or a huge binder full of ideas we can't afford to execute, and then leave. Why don't we, within our businesses and professions, look at ourselves

as "consultants?" We certainly have an advantage over those outsiders —
while we may lack external perspectives and perhaps competitor insights
they might be privy too, *we* know the players in our organization and we
know the product (service) we're trying to sell.

Being an internal consultant — and truly seeing yourself that way — can be an important step in becoming sought-after.

Some examples of proactive, internal consulting:

➤ Marketing professionals should present options on how to
best deliver the message of the company — how to refresh the
brand promises, speak differently to new audiences, revamp the
visuals, and more. Being a true marketing "consultant" in your
business means offering these recommendations before the
president *tasks* you with a rebranding project.

➤ Finance professionals should discuss the various risks of
different spending and investment options with the C-suite. If
there's an innovative and low-friction way to make, keep, or save
more money, finance professionals should be surfacing those
recommendations long before the CEO starts panicking about
the balance sheet.

➤ Quality professionals should discuss the costs associated with
continuous improvement to reduce waste, improve throughput,
and add meaningful features to products and services that
might really "wow" the customers/clients and keep a product or
service profitable and fresh over time. Waiting until hundreds
of customers write negative online reviews about a quality issue
puts you behind the 8 ball.

Seeing yourself as a consultant and a guide can make a huge difference in
the impact you offer, the job satisfaction you feel, and the opportunities
that might open up for you in your career. What a change it made when

I started to accept that mindset about my position. I was more confident in presenting recommendations; frankly, I was more creative as well. I got out of my own "guided by the rules" way and looked for creative ways to solve problems. In doing so, my audience started turning to me more because they knew — "She'll find a way." The more I present and demonstrate this approach, the more I am sought-after for input and the more involved I am in the actual decision-making.

Reflection Question

How do you believe your manager and their manager will begin to look at your input when you begin to *consult* instead of *direct*? What might they say when you begin to discuss options enabling them to make an informed decision with facts, figures, perspectives, and contexts that you have provided to help them make the decision? Being positioned "inside" the company as an employee has no bearing on your ability to be a consulting expert! Use your knowledge to the company's advantage and your own. You'll be amazed at how you will start to be heard, be trusted, and be recognized. And if you're already and external consultant, what can you be doing to make yourself more indispensable to your clients? What kind of ideas and insights can you offer *proactively* without looking like you're trying to sell them something?

What's Next? Putting Your "Sought-After" Strategy into Action

The work you have done up to this point in the book — reading about the building blocks so you can become sought-after — was the easy part. The hard part starts later today, tomorrow, next week, or as soon as you choose to commit to putting your sought-after strategy into action. Every presentation I deliver — whether it's in a client's conference room or from a stage at an event — is developed from a standpoint of "what can you apply *today*" from what I have shared. This book is no different. I want you to get busy using the framework and the ideas shared in this book.

Your next steps require some hard and honest soul-searching. Each Building Block chapter ended by asking how you rate yourself in that area today. When it comes to Building Block #1, you may be a subject-matter expert (SME) today, but we all know there is continuous learning to be done; you won't stay an expert if you don't keep learning. And when you think about Building Block #4, you might realize you have room for growth. Perhaps you have change-management experience but aren't ready to fully embrace change. Look deeply at each of the four building blocks:

- **Know *Your* Stuff** (Be a subject-matter expert)

- **Know *Their* Stuff** (Understand the business)

- **Know Your *Audience*** (Communicate effectively with coworkers and customers)

- **Be *Flexible*** (Embrace change, championing opportunities for improvement)

Which of the four building blocks is your strong suit? Which needs some work? Which needs the *most* work? Self-awareness is critical for moving from discovery to action.

Your Personal Sought-After Plan

Now it's time to design your plan for becoming sought-after. Using the worksheet on the next page, chart your path forward. Choose the area in which you need work. Then build your plan. Determine how (and when) you will work toward improving your skills in that particular area. One thing I can guarantee you, becoming stronger in these four areas will not happen overnight, and you won't rise from "good at your job" to "sought-after for your expertise" quickly. It also will not happen if you do not set a plan into motion, with clear objectives and goals. So, let's get started!

Sought-After Worksheet

1. Which of the following areas of workplace performance do you want to work on? Choose one or two.

    ❑ **Know *Your* Stuff** (Be a subject-matter expert)

    ❑ **Know *Their* Stuff** (Understand the business)

    ❑ **Know Your *Audience*** (Communicate effectively with coworkers and customers)

    ❑ **Be *Flexible*** (Embrace change, championing opportunities for improvement)

2. List 1-3 ways you can begin working on these skills. And commit to a timeframe or date when you will start this personal work.

    _____

    _____

    _____

    _____

3. It's helpful to observe those who already demonstrate the skill(s) you want to work on; seek these people out as mentors. Who do you know (at work or in your personal life) who is strong in the areas where you want to grow? When and how will you go about observing them and learning from them?

    _____

    _____

    _____

    _____

4. What kind of formal professional-development opportunities can you seek that can help you to grow in your areas of focus? Are there any LinkedIn Learning modules that might help you enhance your abilities? Consider relevant courses available at either online or local community colleges. Chambers of Commerce generally provide an assortment of educational

opportunities as well. If your business is a member of the Chamber, you most likely have access to those programs at member rates. The more you look, the more opportunities you will find. Make a list of educational opportunities that you'll look into.

_____

_____

_____

_____

5. While you are laser-focused on developing the one or two skills you have chosen to focus on, be sure to keep the other building blocks in the back of your mind. Look to those who have the knowledge, skills, and abilities in those areas and "follow them" on social media or buy them a cup of coffee in exchange for a conversation. You will quickly find that people with these skills will be more than happy to help you develop as well. Go ahead and make a list of people to follow or meet up with.

_____

_____

_____

_____

A Word About Becoming a "Chief"

The "C-suite" is coveted by so many. "Someday, when I'm the CIO [or CMO, CFO, CHRO, or CEO] ..." is a phrase we've all heard at work from ambitious ladder-climbers aiming to be the "chief" decision-maker in their area of expertise (or over the entire organization). Perhaps you are on track to get there someday, or you have at least dreamed about it. I get it — and there's nothing wrong with having the C-suite as a goal. I coveted it once too. Then I got there. My job and career were not any more satisfying with once I had "chief" responsibilities for HR operations. In fact, it was more stressful and involved more headaches than it was worth. Because being at the top (regardless of the title — many "chief" roles have titles like

VP and director) carries major burdens, can be a little lonely, and often doesn't come with the support one would imagine. I'm a hard worker and I deal with challenging situations every day — that wasn't the problem. Workplace "chiefs," as it turns out, are not necessarily sought-after even within their own industries. They are the ones doing the seeking. Everyone else assumes the chiefs are too busy or too important to be a trusted advisor ... and as such, chief leaders often become untouchable.

My hat is off to you if you want to become a chief. It takes hard work and the building blocks we've explored in this book will help get you there. But ... being a chief just didn't bring me joy[13] — *that* was the problem. I thought it would. Working directly with employees, operations, support personnel — that's what brought me joy. True joy. I encourage you to find your own joy. And to recognize that it rarely comes because of a job title. Doing what you love — where and how you want to do it — will make a difference; it will help you become sought-after because you will be more comfortable in your skin. Arriving at the right place in your career is a gift. There, you'll have joy, you'll have passion, and you'll have energy. And you'll be able to joyfully serve those who seek you out for your expertise.

Reflection Question

Wherever you're headed and however long you think it will be, I hope you will find ways to be joyful in your current role. Maybe it's not exactly where you want to be in the long run, but it would behoove you to make the most of the time, exposure, and experience. What learning can you take away from this position at this time? How are you positioning yourself for the next move? The next move can be within the organization or outside. But be joyful in the present.

---

13 Don't get me wrong. Once I founded my own company, HR Resolutions, and gave myself the title President and CEO, that "chief" seat brought me tremendous joy. The work I do to serve clients, collaborate with my team, and evolve and grow my business is rewarding beyond measure. But being someone else's "chief," inside a big bureaucratic machine, was just never going to be the pinnacle of my career. For some of us, entrepreneurship is a stronger lure. And for others, leading inside a large organization that they don't own is precisely where they are hoping to "top out" their careers. Different strokes for different folks.

Where Do You Go Once You've "Finally Arrived?"

Throughout this book, we've talked about mindset shifts —how to go deeper into your own functional expertise with a commitment to "life-long learning," how to become curious enough to learn a whole lot about your business and industry, how to communicate with people who are very different from you, and how to get on board with changes you don't initially support. Developing the competencies to do all that will put you in a very good position to find yourself being heard, being trusted, and being respected for your expertise.

But what about the people who *don't* fully respect you once you have "arrived?" This is something I spoke about with Kate Colbert, the marketing and higher education expert I interviewed for *Sought-After*. At the time of her interview, Kate had just started attracting a lot of attention for her newest book. She told me:

> "There are people who make you feel like you don't deserve it when the success you earned becomes too big to ignore. Yesterday, my new book was the subject of a feature story in *Forbes*. It was one of the proudest moments of my life. And one of my family members imme-diately 'joked:' 'Don't let your head get too big.'

> "And instantly, I felt smaller and less deserving. But here's the truth — My *reputation* is what will drive people to trust me, and when people *trust* me, I can *help* them. My 'celebrity' in certain circles isn't about arrogance … it's about service. And I can serve more people from a larger stage."

Being "sought-after" isn't always perfect, it's not always what you expect, and it often comes with distinct challenges. Become *too* sought-after, and you risk burnout. And if people are constantly seeking your advice without respecting your time and the value you bring, you can find your-self juggling an endless string of requests to "pick your brain." Giving free advice to the point that you're short on time and feeling taken advantage of is a tough place to find yourself. But most people do become that kind of "popular" on the way to the kind of "sought-after" they're really wishing for. It's flattering but it's exhausting. Don't be afraid to set boundaries, to adjust your goals over time, and to step back from the limelight if being "sought-after" in certain ways aren't all they're cracked up to be.

In the end, this is your journey. You get to define what it means to be heard, trusted, and recognized in your own right. And you get to decide how to use the tools and ideas offered to you in this book. It is my hope that I have helped you to think in new ways about how to prioritize self-awareness as you ascend the leadership ladder, how to set yourself apart from the rest, and how to earn (and keep!) workplace and professional credibility in a skeptical world.

Wherever you are and wherever you're headed, there are smart, accessible ways to command more attention, respect, support, loyalty, and compensation. Mastering the Sought-After Framework allows you to become trusted so you can *do* more, *be* more, *achieve* more, and *serve* more.

I wish you all the influence you seek. Step into the opportunity and shine.

CHAPTER 9

SCENARIOS:
Practicing Your New
"Sought After" Skills

N ow is the time — before you close the pages of this book and get back to work —for you to practice your skills in the four building blocks. Hopefully, you accepted my challenge in the *opening* pages of the book and actually started your *Sought-After* journey here as a sort of "pre-test." If you've done so, then exploring the following scenarios again — one last time — will allow you to evaluate your "lessons learned" after reading the book. But, not to fear if you've held these scenarios until the end of your reading journey. They still serve to test your current skill level. Work through these now and come back to them in the future, as you complete your personal learning plan as well. The scenarios won't change … but you will! Just you wait and see.

SCENARIO #1: The VP and the Cost Reduction

You are responsible for seven different locations for your company, and you report to a relatively new vice president who was brought into the company to affect change, grow market share, and reduce costs in a commodities and service industry. Local management exists within these locations but they report to a corporate headquarters, where you work. The "corporate team" consists of human resources, marketing, accounting, logistics, quality, and compliance (as well as your department, if you work in a function that's not already mentioned). You are on a cross-departmental team assigned to analyze and implement change across the division; the proposed changes can be local or national in scope.

The VP is the chair of the Leadership Team — he is driven, has a big ego, and says he doesn't like "yes people" but demonstrates a different attitude to those who oppose his ideas. He plays favorites. You and the other team members are seasoned in your corporate positions and professions.

The VP announces at the meeting today that we are directed to reduce costs across the organization by 25% within the next 14 days. He provides you with the list of budget "line items" he has identified for elimination or reduction, but the team needs to determine additional items and develop an immediate implementation plan.

Regardless of your specialty (finance, communications, human resources, operations, IT, etc.) you *know* the demand is unrealistic. Above all else, some of his recommendations are counter to the corporate mission, vision, and values.

Using the lines and space below, scribble some ideas about how you might handle this scenario now that you have the *Sought-After* framework to guide you. Use the outline below to spur your thinking.

1. **Note the assumptions you are making in evaluating this scenario.**

2. **Identify your area of expertise (*your* "stuff").**

    a. Document your responsibilities to the VP, the organization, and the team.

    b. What questions do you need to have answered so you can advise the team?

    c. What concerns immediately rise to the top?

4. **Identify the business concerns (*their* "stuff").**

4. **Identify the business concerns (*their* "stuff").**

    a. What is the benefit to the business of creating this committee to explore future change initiatives?

    b. How is this adding/detracting to the success of the company?

3. **Prepare your communications plan (for the *audience*).**

    a. Do you tell the president about the dissension within the team?

    b. How do you address "we've always done it this way and it's worked" when you know that you were hired to dismantle the status quo?

3. **What, if any, change will you implement (i.e., how will you be *flexible* and champion change)?**

    a. How will you support the team? The president? The company?

    b. What steps will you take personally, within the committee, and within the organization?

    _____

    _____

    _____

    _____

    _____

    _____

    _____

    _____

    _____

    _____

    _____

SCENARIO #3: The Boss is a Beloved Bully

You report directly to the president of your company. He is, internally, a bully and a tyrant; as far as he's concerned, your department is a nuisance, and you are just the "head nuisance." But he is wildly successful and popular within the business community and the company is incredibly profitable. His senior vice-president has been with him for more than 10 years and shares with you that he's stopped trying to help this leader see the error of his ways. And, remember, the company is wildly successful.

The president has invited (read "ordered") you to lead an ad-hoc committee geared toward internal branding and culture. He doesn't understand why people keep leaving key positions and thinks you can fix it. After privately rolling your eyes, you accept the challenge. You have invited peers, supervisors, and employees from across the organization to a planning meeting to discuss the mission of this ad-hoc committee on organizational branding and culture. EVERYONE (caps intended) takes the meeting as an opportunity to kvetch about the president. Agenda, no agenda, doesn't matter. This is an all-out venting session! Nothing is accomplished.

The president expects a written summary of the meeting and the action plan by the next day.

1. **Note the assumptions you are making in evaluating this scenario.**

2. **Identify your area of expertise (*your* "stuff").**

    a. What is the functional role you play within the company?

    b. What would/could you contribute as the committee leader?

3. **Identify the business concerns (*their* "stuff").**

    a. What is the benefit to the business of creating this committee?

    b. What was the president's purpose (and expectation) for the initiative and in what ways are those expectations reasonable and addressable?

3. **Prepare your communications plan (for the *audience*).**

   a. Write your report. What have you learned or identified?

   b. What's your "move forward" plan?

3. **What, if any, change will you implement (i.e., be *flexible* and champion change)?**

   d. How will you manage (support *or* counteract) the president's expectations?

5. What steps will you take personally, within the committee, and within the organization?

   _____

   _____

   _____

   _____

   _____

   _____

   _____

   _____

   _____

   _____

   _____

   _____

Acknowledgments

There are so many people to thank ...

God — I am blessed beyond measure and know to whom ultimate credit is owed.

My parents — God rest their souls; they set me on my path of independence and enabled me to be whoever I wanted to be. And to my dad, specifically, for demonstrating work ethic, humility, respect, and integrity.

Barry Young, the best husband ever, is an extraordinary man. He's my best friend; he grounds me; he spoils me terribly; and he believes in me 100%!

Phyllis Webber, Ron McKinley, and **Jerry Hiler** — three leaders who saw something in me a long, long time ago and supported my growth in the "early" years.

Glenn Bembenek, who made me go out and talk to people I didn't know about this funny little idea I had about launching a business.

Sara Kennedy, who encouraged me to write this book and has been a steadfast mentee and mentor.

My staff (past, present, and future), for embracing our mission and enabling me to branch out as a leader, author, and speaker.

The Harrisburg Regional Chamber and **CREDC,** who continue to seek me out to serve and lead.

The PA Chamber, who seeks my input as a trusted advisor on several legislative committees.

Lorman Education Services, whose team trusts me to lead and educate.

Lebanon Valley College, who seeks me out as a mentor and leader for their undergraduates and graduates.

The Society for Human Resource Management (SHRM), who has put me on an international stage, more than once.

Steve Gilliland for writing this book's foreword, for providing early input on the manuscript, and for his support beginning way back at SpeakerU!

Kate Colbert, John Dame, and **Ed Staub** for their input and time in supporting the hypothesis for *Sought-After*, for encouraging me to do good work, and for sharing of themselves during their interviews for this book.

Paul Falcone, Steve Gilliland, Sara Kennedy, **Kate Kohler, Amey Sgrignoli, Terri Swain, John J. "Ski" Sygielski,** and **Warren Zeiser** for being my first readers and endorsers for *Sought-After*.

Maria Diaz from **Order and Ease**, for keeping me on task even when I didn't want to!

Kate Colbert and **George Stevens** at **Silver Tree Publishing** for the late nights and the laughter, and for seeing the author inside me!

About the Author

Karen A. Young capitalizes on her more than 30 years' experience as a leader in human resources and applies her know-how to mentor and grow other leaders.

Karen inspires CEOs, CFOs, and others to fulfill their organizations' missions while strengthening their workforces. She is committed to going the extra mile for clients, helping them build leadership frameworks that result in improved workplace culture and lower HR costs.

Karen is a sought-after speaker, trainer, and author. Her latest book, *Sought-After: How to Be Heard, Be Trusted, and Be Recognized for Your Expertise*, provides a fail-safe formula for career success and social mobility, along with entertaining anecdotes about potentially career-ending moves that became a solid foundation for forward trajectory. Her first book, *Honest and Real: An Essential Guide for Drama-Free Human Resources*, reimagines HR fundamentals in a post-pandemic world while offering advice on effective HR practices that will reduce the daily drama that business leaders experience.

Karen holds degrees from Lebanon Valley College and Saint Francis University, as well as certificates in Strategic HR Management from both The Wharton School of Business and Cornell University. Karen is professionally certified by the HR Certification Institute as a Senior Professional in Human Resources (SPHR) as well as the Society for Human Resource Management as a Senior Certified Professional (SHRM-SCP).

Karen resides in Harrisburg, PA, with her husband and retired racing greyhounds. She is an active member and leader in area business chambers and professional organizations.

Keep in Touch!

🌐 **Learn more about Karen Young, HR Resolutions, and the material in this book:**

SoughtAfterTheBook.com | HRResolutions.com

✉ **Send an email to book Karen as a speaker or start a conversation:**

Karen@HRResolutions.com

Info@KarenAYoung.com

@ **Find, follow, share, and engage on social media:**

LinkedIn.com/in/KarenAYoungAuthor

Facebook.com/KarenAYoungAuthor

Twitter.com/HRResolutions

🎁 **Mail or ship something special to:**

Karen Young
HR Resolutions
4075 Linglestown Rd
PMB 256
Harrisburg PA 17112

📖   **To order books in bulk and learn about quantity discounts:**

Interested in ordering 25 or more copies of *Sought-After* for the high-potential employees at your organization, association, or conference? Send Karen an email at Karen@HRResolutions.com.

Also by Karen A. Young ...

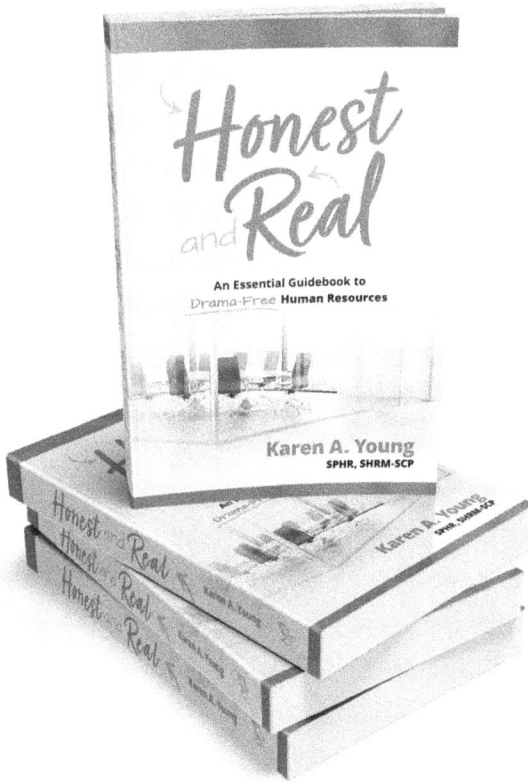

Honest and Real: An Essential Guidebook to Drama-Free Human Resources is an accessible book for business owners, managers, and HR leaders (those with intentional or "accidental" HR responsibility). In this, her first book, Karen shares effective HR systems and practices to help companies reduce incidents, disruptions, and turnover while increasing the bottom line.

In *Honest and Real,* you'll recognize the significant role HR plays in companies of all sizes and learn the benefits of:

➤ Defining expectations

➤ Creating strong job descriptions that drive your HR strategy

➤ Avoiding employment regulatory purgatory

➤ Improving employee morale and retention

Available in paperback and ebook editions.